Making It Happen

Stories
from Inside
the New Workplace

Compiled from
The Systems Thinker™ Newsletter

PEGASUS COMMUNICATIONS, INC.
WALTHAM

Making It Happen: Stories from Inside the New Workplace
Copyright © 1999 by Pegasus Communications, Inc.
First Printing: March 1999

Cataloging-in-Publication Data

Making it happen : stories from inside the new workplace / compiled from *The Systems Thinker* newsletter.
cm.

ISBN 1-883823-32-3 (alk. paper)
1. Organizational change. 2. Leadership. I. Systems Thinker.
HD58.8.M245 1999
658.4'06—dc21   98-48877
                                                                     CIP

Acquiring editor: Kellie Wardman O'Reilly
Project editor: Lauren Johnson
Cover Design: Fineline Communications
Interior Design: Thompson-Steele Production Services
Production: Julie Quinn

Pegasus Communications, Inc. is dedicated to providing resources that help people explore, understand, articulate, and address the challenges they face in managing the complexities of a changing world. Since 1989, Pegasus has worked to build a community of organizational learning practitioners through newsletters, books, audio and video tapes, and its annual *Systems Thinking in Action*® Conference and other events. For additional copies or information on volume discounts, contact:

Pegasus Communications, Inc.
One Moody Street
Waltham, MA 02453-5339
PEGASUS   Phone: (781) 398-9700 Fax: (781) 894-7175
COMMUNICATIONS   www.pegasuscom.com

♻ Printed on recycled paper.

05   04   03   02   01   00   99   10   9   8   7   6   5   4   3   2   1

5138

Acknowledgments

Thank you to all the individuals who are using the principles, tools, and disciplines of organizational learning to meet the workplace challenges of today and to anticipate the emerging challenges of tomorrow. In particular, thanks to the contributing authors of *Making It Happen* for their valuable efforts to show us how to implement change, and for sharing their keen insights. This book would not exist without their passion, clarity, and commitment.

The chapters in this book first appeared in *The Systems Thinker*™ Newsletter and were edited by Kellie Wardman O'Reilly, Colleen Lannon, Janice Molloy, and Lauren Johnson, with support from Daniel H. Kim.

HOW TO READ CAUSAL LOOP DIAGRAMS

As you read the chapters in this book, you'll notice that many of them contain diagrams featuring circular arrows and labels such as "R," "s," and so forth. These causal loop diagrams consist of variables connected by arrows that show the movement of feedback through the system. Each arrow is labeled with a sign ("s" or "o") that indicates how one variable influences another. Here's an example of a simple CLD:

In this diagram, stress level and use of coping mechanisms are the two variables connected by feedback arrows. The "s" on the upper arrow means that when the stress level changes, the use of coping mechanisms changes in the *same* direction. For example, if the stress level increases, the use of coping mechanisms also increases. The "o" on the lower arrow means that when use of coping mechanisms changes, then the level of stress changes in the *opposite* direction. For instance, as use of coping mechanisms increases, the stress level decreases.

Causal loop diagrams are made up of a combination of balancing and reinforcing loops. The CLD we just "walked through" is an example of a balancing loop, as indicated by the "B" in the center. A balancing process tends to keep the system behavior relatively steady overall. In our example, for instance, the two variables balance each other and keep each other under control.

A reinforcing process, by contrast, drives change in one direction with even more change. Reinforcing processes are recognizable by the uncontrolled or exponential changes that they create. The figure below, labeled "R," is a simple example of this kind of dynamic.

In this reinforcing loop, each arrow is labeled with an "s" for same direction of change. To read this diagram, you would say that "as marketing increases, so do sales, which leads to more funds available for marketing, which leads to even more marketing."

Balancing and reinforcing processes occur in infinite combinations in the systems we see all around us, including behavior within organizations.

HOW TO READ STOCK AND FLOW DIAGRAMS

In addition to the causal loop diagrams in this book, you'll also notice other kinds of diagrams that consist of circles, boxes, arrows, and cloudlike objects. These are called stock and flow diagrams, and are another device for representing systems.

To read one of these diagrams, you first need to know what stocks and flows are. Stocks (often called accumulators) are anything that accumulate and that can be measured at one point in time, such as population, the amount of water in a bathtub, and so on. Flows represent things that change over time, such as number of births, the inflation rate, etc.

Unlike causal loops, stock and flow diagrams provide information about rates of change. In brief, they show how the various stocks and flows in the system influence one another and how the feedback flows through the system.

These diagrams are also often used to build computer simulation models; the model builder assigns initial values to the stocks (such as "population equals 2,000 at time zero") and rates for the flows (such as "20 births per month").

The diagram below identifies the various parts of a stock and flow diagram.

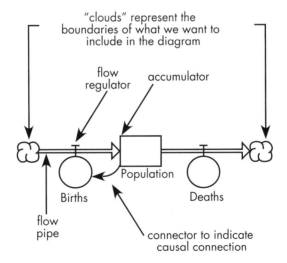

Contents

Part Three   *Transforming People and Culture*

The Power of Story

"The story's about you."

—Quintus Horatius Flaccus,
Satires, Book 1, 35 B.C.

Quintus Horatius Flaccus—the Roman poet and satirist more commonly known as Horace—had a deep insight into the power of story that holds just as true today as it did back in 35 B.C. Stories are powerful because, no matter who the characters are or what the setting, stories are about *us*. Stories exert a profound influence: They draw us in, and they transform our sense of time, place, and identity. By listening to or reading a story, we see ourselves in the characters and learn what we, too, might become under a new set of circumstances. Through the telling of a story, we share lessons that might be of great benefit to others, and we illuminate important truths.

Making It Happen: Stories from Inside the New Workplace seeks to evoke the special power of story. In this collection, each contributing author has experienced a journey into organizational learning that proved so impactful that he or she felt compelled to share it. Whether the setting is a large corporation, a small division within a big company, a healthcare organization, or a school or classroom, the stories herein open a window onto how real people in real organizations go about creating the new workplace. Such stories are not always about success. Many of these authors—keenly aware that we learn just as much from our disappointments as we do from our achievements—tell about failures as well.

The stories also reveal the deep and varied sense of purpose infusing these efforts. For example, in Part I, "Launching Large-Scale Change," we meet change leaders who recognized that their entire organization had to transform itself in order to navigate the ever-shifting waters of business life. Companies like Shell Oil, Chrysler, Philips Display Components, and others share dramatic accounts of both the promise and the pitfalls of incorporating widespread change. In Part II, "Addressing Critical Business Challenges," we see examples of more focused change—for example, the U.S. Navy's redesign of its acquisition process, Kellogg Brown & Root's new idea for improving team learning through debriefing projects, Arthur Andersen Business Consulting's quest to improve client satisfaction, and many others. Finally, in Part III, "Transforming People and Culture," we "zoom in" even closer to see how several organizations have addressed one particularly daunting challenge: reshaping their culture. This section contains an especially rich blend of organizations, ranging from a technical college to a nonprofit to a large high-tech firm.

Whatever their setting or individual purpose, these authors all have one thing in common: They wanted to make their organizations more effective and more humane places to be.

The stories in *Making It Happen* offer another, equally valuable benefit: They show, in action, the broad range of tools and methods for change developed by the organizational learning community. From causal loop diagrams to systems archetypes and stock and flow diagrams, from simulation modeling to Human Dynamics and dialogue, all these tools have a power and a promise that can be found only in this community.

And finally, one of the nice things about stories is that they have a way of inspiring more stories. So, we invite you to open this book and discover for yourself how the selections within might spark your own ideas for transforming your organization. We hope you will then turn those ideas into action, and begin generating your own stories about organizational learning in the new workplace.

—The Editors of *The Systems Thinker*™

Part One

Launching
Large-Scale
Change

What do you do when you realize that, to navigate the ever-shifting waters of business life, your entire organization or division needs to be transformed? Where do you begin? In this section, change leaders from Chrysler Corporation, Ford Motor Company, Philips Display Components, and others share their experiences in launching change initiatives both broadly and deeply throughout the organization. The distinguishing theme in all of these accounts is that these companies—whether an industrial giant like Shell Oil or a publicly owned utility company such as Cleveland Public Power—sought to extend change into the farthest corners of their organization.

Many of these stories are ongoing even today, as the companies featured in them continue to evolve through their learning journey. Their successes, as well as their failures, offer profound lessons about the nature of widespread change in the new workplace.

Chapter One

Organizational Learning at Philips Display Components

by Iva M. Wilson

W hat are the potential gains and pitfalls of launching an organizational learning initiative in a company whose governance model has historically been "top-down"? The story of Philips Display Components captures the drama inherent in this sort of journey. Philips Display Components (PDC) makes the color cathode ray tubes that are used in television sets. Located in the U.S., the company is owned by Philips, which is headquartered in the Netherlands. In the 1980s, PDC had about 2,500 employees and $250 million in sales. It also had several daunting problems. Smarting from undercapitalization from its former owner and a stiffening of foreign competition, it decided to launch a series of change efforts in 1986 that eventually led it to explore the principles and tools of organizational learning. In 1992, PDC became a sponsoring company of the Organizational Learning Center at MIT, which offered a five-day core course, project assistance from researchers and consultants associated with MIT, and interaction with other sponsoring companies. The objective was to gradually expose PDC employees to the tools described in Peter Senge's book *The Fifth Discipline* and to teach them how to apply those tools to their work.

Selecting Participants in the Change Effort

In March 1992, the company invited nine PDC managers to attend the OLC's core course, which covers the various tools of organizational learning. The goal was to then introduce the initiative gradually to a diagonally cross-functional group of people, who could take the change process further and engage the rest of the organization. To that end, the management team decided to make participation in the core course voluntary. As we will see, this decision had some undesirable consequences.

Applying Learning Tools

As people began attending the OLC course, the PDC management team encouraged them to use organizational learning tools in all aspects of their work, such as in the strategic planning process, product development, and so forth. These tools included dialogue, which helps participants surface and share mental models; balancing advocacy and inquiry, which fosters generative conversation; the left-hand/right-hand column, which enhances people's ability to navigate difficult conversations; and the ladder of inference, which helps people understand how their assumptions about the world shape their behavior. In addition, participants began to explore systems thinking tools, including behavior over time graphs, which reveal changes in key variables; causal loop diagrams, which show the systemic structures that generate behavior patterns; and simulation modeling, which shows how business decisions play out over time.

The people who were most familiar with these tools became champions of them, introducing others to the tools and encouraging use of the tools throughout the organization. As they went about this process, it soon became clear that the more technical tools of systems thinking, such as simulation modeling, were not being employed nearly as much as the other tools. Again, this development would lead to problems later.

Encountering Obstacles to Organizational Learning

By 1994, PDC was investing liberally in organizational learning training opportunities. The company struggled with many challenges in implementing the ideas, however. For example, after Philips had acquired PDC in 1983, a volatile mix of cultures had arisen at PDC that created tensions throughout the managerial layer. There was the culture of Philips itself, which reflected the direct, sometimes blunt communication style often used in the Netherlands. There was also a sense of an "old-guard" culture owing to the presence of several individuals who had been with PDC since before Philips acquired it. Moreover, there were the cultures of at least two competitors from where a number of new senior managers came. For example, one manager came from Zenith Radio Corporation, which operated with a "can-do" attitude, loose management structure, and the assumption that talented people could grow through the ranks. Other senior managers came from RCA, a highly structured American company that had won a reputation as the "father of TV" and that competed fiercely with Philips to retain this reputation. And as in any big company, there were subcultures defined by regional location and function.

In the fall of 1994, a major challenge arose. After difficult negotiations over some changes that management had proposed to their contract, the company's unionized workforce decided to go on strike. Though traumatic, the strike gave PDC an opportunity to practice using some of its new organizational learning tools. Everyone—managers, salaried workers, and union members—needed to grasp how their actions had precipitated this event. A meeting of 60 people, from PDC's headquarters and its factory, was called to explore the forces behind the strike through the use of dialogue. This emotional gathering yielded many profound insights. For example, the group uncovered deep resentments between the salaried and unionized work forces, as well as disagreements on union policies *within* the unionized work force.

Amazingly, no one lost his or her job during this grueling analysis. Moreover, through the use of dialogue especially, the participants were able to avoid casting blame despite the intensely painful issues being discussed. Indeed, as early as the next spring, PDC had reopened the union contract negotiations and succeeded in outlining a new agreement.

Deep Divisions at Philips

Despite this successful resolution, concerns about both the strike and the tensions within the management team still simmered. Early in 1995, a three-day managers' offsite was held to discuss these issues. As a result of these discussions, the team decided to launch a project to assess organizational issues within PDC as well as PDC's relationship to the global Philips business. Differences of opinion among management about how PDC should be organized—in particular, whether the factory should be more independent from PDC headquarters—had created a profound rift between the parent company's and PDC's leadership. The primary objective of the offsite was to come to agreement about how PDC would be organized.

The offsite revealed just how deep the divisions in management were. After a four-month-long effort to reorganize PDC along the lines of the parent company, PDC's and Philips' top management simply reached an impasse. Refusing to approve the organizational structure that PDC's leadership proposed, Philips decreed that PDC would be allowed to implement only the recommendations that the parent company saw fit.

What Happened? A Closer Look at the PDC Experience

The learning initiative at PDC scored some successes. However, in many ways, it fell victim to some inherent systemic structures at work in the company.

Assumptions About Change. One of these problematic systemic structures involved the assumptions that people at PDC made about the change effort. As in numerous large companies, the PDC learning initiative was seen by many as mere "cultural, OD stuff." In addition, the decision to make participation in the training voluntary led to a lack of balance in the organization members' appreciation of the various learning disciplines. Because participation was voluntary, the effort attracted people who already had an affinity for organizational improvement and the idea of vision. Seeing the purpose of the learning initiative as an opportunity to work toward a shared vision rather than to solve a specific problem, these participants tended to be more drawn to tools such as dialogue and team learning rather than systems thinking, modeling, and some of the other more technical tools. Over time, the situation began to resemble a version of the "Success to the Successful" systems archetype, in which one set of tools began to gain more support than the other set (see "Success to the 'Softer' Tools"). Eventually, some of the more technical high-level managers dismissed the learning effort as too "soft" and declined to support it. Even though the learning initiative spread at first, it could not be sustained without widespread support and was ultimately abandoned when a new president came on board.

SUCCESS TO THE "SOFTER" TOOLS

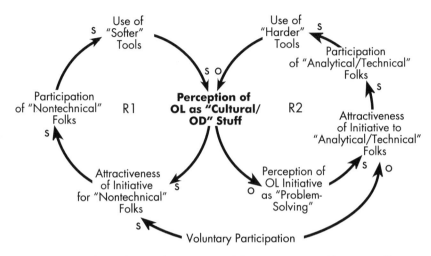

Because of a widespread perception of the organizational learning effort as mere "OD stuff," the initiative tended to attract mostly people who had an affinity for the "softer" tools of OL, which reinforced the original perception (R1). As this perception grew, people began to see the initiative as less effective for "real" problem-solving. The more technical/analytical employees ignored the initiative, and use of "harder" tools declined—further reinforcing the perception of the initiative as too "soft" (R2).

Source: Don Seville

"Worse Before Better." Another problematic structure for PDC involves the well-known tendency of things to get "worse before better" as an organization begins implementing change. During such times, a change initiative becomes very vulnerable. At PDC, as people began using OL tools in the early stages of the learning initiative, a sense of openness began to build within the company (see "Worse Before Better" on p. 10). People felt increasingly secure in sharing their opinions about and criticisms of the new initiative. Eventually, as they also mastered new communication skills through the application of OL tools, these disagreements would have tapered off because the participants would have begun addressing the real roots of conflict through their use of the new skills (B4 and the behavior over time graph).

Unfortunately for PDC, Philips took action before the "worse" could turn into the "better." During the delay in which communication skills were ramping up (B4), the freely delivered feedback (even though it was conveyed with the best intentions) alarmed Philips' top management, who decided that PDC was "out of control" (B5). Top Philips management thus began intervening in PDC's learning initiative, choking off the fragile culture of openness that PDC had begun to build, and effectively reducing the voicing of disagreements. If PDC had been able to explain this dynamic and the ramifications of delay to Philips, the Philips managers may not have acted so hastily. Ironically, the voicing of disagreements that Philips found so disturbing would then have petered out on its own eventually.

WORSE BEFORE BETTER

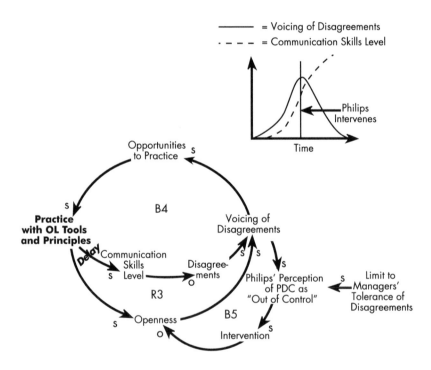

The increased voicing of disagreements that resulted from the climate of openness that PDC began creating through its learning initiative alarmed Philips' top managers, who intervened in the initiative and reversed the progress of PDC's learning initiative.

Source: Don Seville

Power and Authority. Power is the ability to do and act; authority is the right to control and command. Every individual in an organization can do and act, while only certain individuals have the right to control and command. As in most hierarchical organizations, managers at PDC found it difficult to begin sharing power. The act of assuming power can also be frightening to many people, because it means added responsibility, risk, and accountability. Organizational learning can help overcome this reluctance. Once people have learned something, they are in a stronger position to take on power because their new knowledge has lessened the risks involved. However, this process takes time. If Philips had been better able to tolerate the delays in the organizational learning journey, PDC might have had more success encouraging a sharing of power.

Epilogue

After leaving PDC in 1995, I took a position as senior vice president of manufacturing technology for Philips U.S. My successor back at PDC did not support the learning initiative there, and the effort died out. However, at Philips U.S., new opportunities arose to continue exploring the use of organizational learning tools and principles. Specifically, Philips' U.S. Manufacturing Council developed a new manufacturing training program that featured many of the organizational learning disciplines and tools. The program, which emphasized change management, among other skills, consisted of classroom work as well as active practice and learning laboratory activities. It was delivered to local Philips manufacturing supervisors on site across the U.S. Participants attended courses for five days (one of which focused on change management and organizational learning tools), learned to apply their new skills at work over the next few months, and then attended subsequent rounds of courses.

This program—especially the change management portion—continues to be successful even today. Participants express much enthusiasm about what they are learning and maintain that the program has helped them manage both their jobs and people more effectively. In addition, managers have learned to become less controlling, and there is more joint understanding of current reality. Perhaps the most satisfying outcome is that this module has earned the highest scores from attendees.

Was PDC's experience with organizational learning a "success" or a "failure"? The question is difficult to answer. Even though PDC couldn't clearly show a correlation between practice of the learning disciplines and an increase in profitability, the company did see a desirable change in teams who practiced the learning disciplines. Individuals gained a stronger sense of their own contribution to current reality and learned to see the world differently. People also learned to reframe issues, help others to clarify their perspectives, and engage in tense discussion with less blaming than before. Finally, and perhaps most important, the learning effort—both its successes and its failures—yielded important insights about the nature of change that are pertinent and valuable for any organization. ↝

Iva M. Wilson is the retired president of Philips Display Components, where she served in that role from 1986 to 1996. She has also participated in the design team that created the Society for Organizational Learning (SoL) and was appointed SoL's first president, a post that she held until the end of 1997. She serves as a board member of The Environmental Research Institute of Michigan and of Michigan Future Inc.

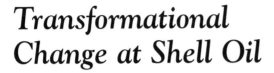

Transformational Change at Shell Oil

by Phil Carroll

T he change effort at Shell Oil began back in 1991 and 1992, in response to serious problems of underperformance. Namely, the company was riddled with operational difficulties, unprofitable investments, and low morale resulting from massive layoffs. After one particularly bad round of layoffs in late 1991 that impacted the administrative functions—finance, information services, etc.—morale in these groups was especially low. It was clear that we had to make large-scale changes if we were going to get back on track.

At that time, I decided to go out and talk individually with every person in those departments. As you can imagine, it's a sobering experience to stand up in front of people who have lost trust in you. I had to explain to them, in all candor, that I had in fact participated in a lot of the decisions that had led to the financial problems that produced the layoffs.

Remarkably, this simple admission not only helped me see things from their perspective, but it began to release some of the frustration, bitterness, and immobilization that had arisen in these departments. People knew they were in just as much jeopardy as they had been before, but they had begun to feel once again that they, and the company, had the power to rebound.

These meetings also raised a key question: *How do you help a group of people discover for themselves what is necessary in order to succeed collectively?* This is a core theme behind any change work—and it's what Shell set about trying to do. True, there were a lot of problems with the culture of Shell Oil at the time. We were bureaucratic, hierarchical, numbers-driven, linear thinkers. But we were also blessed with high-quality people: people who were willing to do whatever was necessary to ensure the success of their business unit and the company, and who felt a strong commitment to excellence and to personal improvement. We had to find ways to fix our problems while sustaining and cultivating these strengths.

Reeducating the Management Team

In the early summer of 1993, several events occurred that generated ideas about how we might institute such a radical change. First, a series of off-site meetings among the administrative vice presidents got us thinking about the possible root causes of Shell's troubles. A second offsite, a facilitated gathering of upper management, got us talking about the changes that we wanted to make. This offsite revealed a key failing: None of us had even the simplest skills for talking to each other in a meaningful way. We could debate with each other extremely well, but we could not sit down and listen, nor could we share what we were thinking about with each other. We were loaded with dysfunctional behavior that we had picked up from our professional training.

This offsite revealed a key failing: None of us had even the simplest skills for talking to each other in a meaningful way.

Yet we struggled on. Our facilitators helped us to begin surfacing problems, laying out our real feelings about them, and listening to each others' ideas without concluding that we had to surrender our own. We also began to recognize that the management team lacked real business acumen. We were all engineers or scientists, and we thought about things in scientific and operational terms without being able to link those things to business realities and results.

Clearly, we had to reeducate ourselves, to develop a business-model methodology and put it in place throughout the company. We called together the top 200 people in Shell Oil Company in February 1994 to begin addressing these key questions: What was the company's vision? What did we want to become? What values did we need to practice in order to achieve whatever vision we finally agreed on?

We started by trying to arrive at the most basic kind of alignment that one can have in a large organization—a shared view of where we wanted to go, as well as a common understanding of where we stood relative to that vision. Then we worked on clarifying our values. In the end, our vision statement read that we strived to be the premier U.S. company with sustained world-class performance in all aspects of the business. Our list of core values included belief in people, excellence, sense of urgency, trustworthiness, and innovation.

Clearly, we had to reeducate ourselves, to develop a business-model methodology and put it in place throughout the company.

Yet when we tried to "roll out" the vision-and-values statement to the rest of the company, people either ignored it or expressed skepticism. It's not that the vision was bad, or that the value system was inconsistent with the way people believed. But there were several "disconnects" between the stated, desired value system and reality. For example, even though people truly wanted to be innovative, in reality, initiating change was very risky at Shell during these years.

Still, the organization was fundamentally ripe for the kind of change that we were beginning to talk about. As we improved our change-management skills, we began engaging more and more people throughout Shell in generating ideas for how to implement the vision and values. We also asked a focusing question: What do we really believe in? We realized that we had three fundamental beliefs, and based on those beliefs, we put forth three challenges to everyone at Shell.

Three Beliefs and Three Challenges

The first belief—"People are good"—may not seem like a deep idea, but it has profound connotations for how people act with each other and the kinds of assumptions we each make about each other. The second belief was: "People are capable." They can be trusted to do the right thing—and more—if they know what the right thing is. The third belief was: "Market systems work." If you apply market principles to an organization, then these principles will produce the results you want.

As we continued to engage people in exploring these ideas, we began asking everyone—whether a newly hired secretary or a top executive—to do three things. First, we asked that everybody think about and perform their job just as if they were a publicly held company of one. This meant reflecting on what their "product" was and who their "customers" and "competitors" were, and identifying competitors—whether within or outside Shell—who could provide their product or their service more cheaply or effectively. It also meant keeping a constant eye out for new products or services that might be worth developing.

Second, we asked people to aim for the highest level of professional excellence they could. That is, with the help of the company, they had to shoulder the responsibility for strengthening their own skills and for understanding the various ways they might add value to the business.

Third, we urged people to be a constructive force for change in the corporation rather than passively seeking shelter in the company. This meant attending workshops on change skills, engagement skills, and business-model application; incorporating 360-degree feedback and discussion of Shell's vision and values into performance reviews; and adding a component to pay scales that hinged on business performance.

Establishing New Governance Structures

In early 1995, we took our next major step: installing new structures at the upper management level designed to strengthen the leadership skills of those at lower levels. To this end, we established separate business units within Shell. Each unit agreed on a balance sheet and a debt structure and had its own board of directors. In essence, we set up the major organizations within Shell just as if they—like the individuals within them—were publicly held companies. These new units in turn established additional subsidiary companies within their organizations. In this way, the principle of subsidiarity, of pushing these levels of responsibility down, penetrated throughout the business.

The release of creative energy that came with this new governance structure and the philosophy behind it led to a remarkable resurgence of entrepreneurial spirit. People also felt a new sense of responsibility and self-discipline in the way they dealt with capital. Now, each unit was free to

---

This new governance structure led to a remarkable resurgence of entrepreneurial spirit.

---

take on new projects—but they also had to find a way to pay for them. They began to think twice about how they wanted to spend money. This is a powerful example of how the strict application of a well-understood business-model methodology allows people to run their business but at the same time holds them accountable for its performance. As a result, all of us were now answerable for what happened in our organizations. Decision-making began taking place throughout the ranks, rather than only at the highest levels.

Developing New Leadership Skills and Business Acumen

In addition to these structural changes, we had another offsite gathering of senior management, during which we further clarified our desired process of change. In adopting a new leadership model, we didn't just want people with important-sounding titles; we wanted everyone in the company to recognize the necessity of exercising leadership in their job. We saw that we had to set up a learning center, a place where we could begin imparting the characteristics of this leadership style and provide a practice field for people to try applying these principles in their actual jobs.

We also set out to improve the ability of all Shell employees to engage one another in meaningful conversation. This too involved the teaching of certain basic principles and the provision of a practice field where people could come together and learn by doing. The goal was for people to discover how to address difficult problems openly, cooperatively, and in a spirit of community rather than dominance.

Finally, we sought to expand the concept of the business model, which we hoped would help people see where value is created in the company and identify customers' needs. Each of us had to improve our performance to the utmost on these fundamental value drivers.

We believed that if we did all this—developed leadership capacity, honed communication skills, and adopted a disciplined business methodology that let people look accurately at how the business was performing— we could then get at the central element of all of this: the alignment of people throughout the company (see "Alignment at Shell"). By alignment, we meant that we would each be clear about the direction we wanted to head in. We would also know the methodologies by which we would get there. And, we would each have the freedom to act.

Shell Achieves a Critical Mass

We continued down this path through 1995 and 1996, including building the new learning center. We also assembled a business

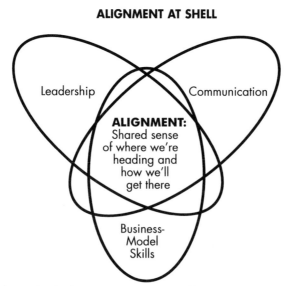

ALIGNMENT AT SHELL

Leadership

Communication

ALIGNMENT:
Shared sense
of where we're
heading and
how we'll
get there

Business-
Model
Skills

By developing leadership, communication, and business-model skills, Shell worked to foster a shared sense of where the organization was heading and how it would get there.

transformation team consisting of some of the best and brightest young people from the company. They fanned out and tried to help other parts of the company begin to apply the new leadership concepts in actual business circumstances.

In late 1996/early 1997, things began to shift dramatically in the company. The cynicism and skepticism began to evaporate as a sufficient number of people took ownership of the underlying concepts and began to conduct their affairs differently. Over the next 18 months, it seemed that this process accelerated.

Does that kind of shift come about because of some intervention from above, or because the company reaches a critical mass in terms of the numbers of people embracing the idea of change? This is a difficult question to answer. What *is* clear is that things were never the same after that period. To this day, no matter whom you ask in the company, people know what "transformation" is about. They know the fundamentals.

> *To this day, no matter whom you ask in the company, people know what "transformation" is about.*

They know about business models. They know that leadership is engaging them in the decision-making process and inviting them to make better use of their talents.

Progress on this front also translated into strong financial results. In 1997, Shell set another record when its net income hit $2,104 million. Moreover, its operating cashflow proved strong enough to support a $3.5 billion investment program and competitive dividends to shareholders. Shell's healthy balance sheet enabled the company to pursue and close strategic acquisitions totaling in excess of $2.8 billion.

Moreover, the new ideas percolating at Shell not only moved through Shell Oil Company but also gained momentum in the European, Asian, and other locations of Shell's parent company, Royal Dutch/Shell. Today, the entire Royal Dutch/Shell Group is immersed in a process of transformation. At one pivotal conference held in the spring of 1998, 600 senior leaders from around the world came together in the Netherlands to discuss the Group's overall direction, share experiences, learn, and leverage best practices. The conference, which lasted four days, revealed a deep commitment to the principles of transformation. Attendees clarified the Group's sense of purpose—"to help people build a better world"—and explored ideas for tapping into the depth of talent in the Group, including leveraging the power of virtual and cross-functional teams. "Everywhere there was interest in building the capacity for organizational learning," one attendee wrote, "to accelerate our ability to learn, both individually and collectively."

Clearly, transformative change was accelerating not only throughout Shell Oil Company but also throughout the much larger international community of which it was a part.

Reflections on Shell's New Leadership Model

Shell's story of organizational learning raises several themes about leadership that are both timely and universal to any organization seeking to transform itself. Below is a brief exploration of each of these themes.

The Challenge of Shared Leadership. Shell made huge strides in moving from a command-and-control leadership model to one of shared leadership. Yet the process has not been easy. Many leaders have had real difficulty giving up command-and-control and trusting people enough to empower them to make decisions. Some of them have also feared that the new governance model would result in the loss of their own positions.

To address these fears, the senior leaders who were championing the change have had to do two things: keep serving as living examples of the transformation, and keep supporting progress in this area, rather than castigating people for stumbling as they try to adopt the new model.

For shared leadership to truly work, one key is that people have to trust that their own supervisors truly want to see them act in a new way. One method for building this trust is to explain that devolving power does not mean total anarchy. Indeed, there are certain minimum conditions that must be in place for shared leadership to succeed (see "Three

Conditions for Devolving Power"). The first condition—and the one where leadership quite often fails—is clarity about the common objective. Leaders can play an important role in helping people gain such clarity by continuously engaging people in business strategies and the underlying business model. If this is handled skillfully, each person begins to see his or her own part in adding value to the business.

The second condition is that people have to have the capacity to do what you're asking them to do. There are some tasks that require very specific experience and the building of certain skills. If you haven't provided people with the training and education they need to handle empowerment, then you're not doing right by them, and the effort is bound to fall flat.

The third condition is that with empowerment comes a much higher degree of accountability for both desirable and undesirable results. If I am empowered, I make choices based on my skills. If a decision doesn't turn out well, I have to be held accountable for that. There has to be an explicit process in place for clarifying that accountability. Shell has made a lot of progress in that regard, and a lot of the credit belongs to senior leaders who have begun to "walk the talk" of devolving power and to middle managers who have picked up on the idea.

Resistance to Change: The "Clay Layer" of Management. At Shell, the transformation effort was eventually embraced by the top 200 people of the company. Our next challenge was to address what I call the "clay layer" in the organization—those managers who for 20 or 30 years had been rewarded for their more traditional approaches to leadership.

It's easy to think of that group as an impervious "clay" layer at which corporate cultural change efforts stop abruptly. But is that really the problem? My belief is that these people are just as eager as the change

---

THREE CONDITIONS FOR DEVOLVING POWER

1. Everyone agrees on and shares the company's overall objective.
2. People have the training, education, and skills to handle local decision-making.
3. The company has an explicit structure in place for holding people accountable for the results of their decisions.

champions to see the emergence of a work environment that encourages creativity and that gives people the freedom to both succeed and fail. However, oftentimes higher managers are not modeling the new leadership consistently, and are therefore presenting mixed messages to leaders below them. In addition, high-level managers frequently fail to provide enough protection and encouragement for those below them who are trying to change.

To address these obstacles, Shell took a multipronged approach to support this leadership community. First, the Shell learning center designed and delivered workshops on the new leadership model. In addition, the company incorporated a new policy of 360-degree feedback. Finally, Shell introduced a pay-for-performance policy to reward managers who succeeded in adopting the new leadership model.

When a Leader Leaves. At Shell, the question of "what will happen once Phil is gone" had been discussed in get-togethers throughout the company for about a year before my retirement date. Everybody knew the rules of the game about retirement age. Of course, a central question

---

At Shell, the progress we've made is very likely to be sustained, because the ideas behind it are right.

---

in this sort of transition becomes, Is our progress going to evaporate once the leader leaves? This in turn leads to questions about how deeply and broadly a change is institutionalized, and about how much other leaders are "walking the talk."

At Shell, the progress we've made is very likely to be sustained, because the ideas behind it are right. There are also sufficient numbers of people in the company now who share a commitment to the change that it is very likely to be carried on. Finally, there have been enough senior leaders who have come forth and taken a personal stand on these principles, values, and beliefs. It's going to be very difficult for somebody new to come in and wipe away our achievements.

But this isn't an excuse to stop being vigilant: What we've achieved *can* be destroyed. All it takes is certain behaviors to begin to shift people to a less effective mode. However, my successor is both a strong believer and a good practitioner of these same principles. Given both his and others' leadership throughout the company, this transformational process is bound to continue.

The business transformation team we put in place is another reason to have hope for the future. This team consists of 15 or so extremely bright people who have been serving as in-house consultants at Shell for about four years. They are steeped in the principles and practices of the transformation. Most of the first-generation members of this team are now on other business assignments throughout the company. Their influence in supporting and spreading this change process is impossible to overestimate.

The Locus of Change—Today and Tomorrow

The theme of shared leadership brings up the question of where true change resides. Does change have to initiate from the top and then be sustained from middle and lower levels? At Shell, the transformation effort in some ways looked like a top-down process. True, the people at the top were *supportive* of change. However, the changes themselves—important modifications to behaviors and attitudes—were made by people throughout the ranks in the company.

Also, there were a number of places within Shell Oil where people had been on this road long before I ever came along or had anything to say about it. They simply knew that this was the right way to do things. The key is to keep the conversation about the change process going—with all levels of management, with change champions, and with individual contributors who want to support the transformation.

Shell's investment in transformation has done just this—by building both individuals' and the collective's ability to meet new challenges. As Shell's business portfolio continues to become more globalized, the transformations both within Shell and throughout the parent company, Royal Dutch/Shell, are growing more and more closely aligned. This strikingly synchronistic phenomenon holds both promise and challenges for the century ahead. ⌁

Phil Carroll served as president and CEO of Shell Oil Company from July 1993 to June 1998. His tenure at Shell began in 1961 and included service as an engineer, vice president of public affairs, managing director of Shell International Gas, senior vice president of administration, and executive vice president. He has a deep commitment to community service and, to that end, serves on a number of civic and charitable boards nationally. A native of New Orleans, he holds a B.S. degree in physics from Loyola University and an M.S. degree in physics from Tulane University. He and his wife, Charlene, have three children and two grandchildren.

This chapter was adapted from an address given by Phil Carroll, on the eve of his retirement from Shell, at the 1998 Annual Members' Meeting of the Society for Organizational Learning, in Amherst, Massachusetts.

Facing the Competition: An Organization Mobilizes for Large-Scale Change

by Nagah Ramadan and Patrick Parker-Roach

Cleveland Public Power is the municipal electric power company for the city of Cleveland, Ohio. Since its founding in 1908, CPP has been locked in a bitter, competitive battle with an investor-owned electric utility. The two companies compete on a street-by-street, house-by-house basis. In fact, it is not unusual to see two sets of power poles lining the same street.

In 1987, CPP was funded by a large bond issue and decided to use the funding to expand its coverage across the city. As a result of this effort, the company's service area expanded from 35 percent to nearly 50 percent between 1987 and 1995. Although the physical effort of putting up poles, stringing cable, and installing meters on homes progressed well, CPP began feeling growing pains. And although customer *demand* remained high throughout the expansion effort, customer *satisfaction* ratings fell. CPP's operating systems and organizational structures simply could not keep pace with the company's expanding power delivery system and increases in customer demand.

Addressing the Growth Problem: First Steps

Early in 1995, the mayor of Cleveland appointed a new commissioner to address these growth problems. The commissioner immediately embarked on a major transformation effort not only to address CPP's performance issues but also to maneuver the company into position to handle another looming challenge: the deregulation of the electric power industry. The company launched the change effort by conducting an "assessment of current reality" in March–April 1995 that led to an action plan for the transformation of CPP.

Assembling the Team. The commissioner realized that if CPP wanted to achieve sustainable transformation, the people who would have to implement the change and live with the results must also be able to embrace it. He assembled a change team comprising a complete cross-section of CPP's population. It included managers and line workers from each major function of the company, and reflected a balance of gender, union membership, seniority, and other factors. CPP also engaged two outside process facilitators to guide the team through the assessment effort.

Preparing for the Assessment. The facilitators then conducted one-on-one, confidential interviews with the 35 members of the assessment team, so as to get a sense of CPP's culture and any concerns or problems that may have been lurking under the surface. Next, the team played The Beer Game, which showed them how systemic structure drives behavior in organizations. The new, shared understandings that arose from playing the game set a tone of openness and warded off the all-too-common tendency to blame others for organizational problems.

Analyzing Current Reality

Now came the real "meat" of the process. To assess current conditions at CPP, the team engaged in four distinct steps:

1. Detailing functional activities
2. Analyzing functional relationships
3. Performing a root-cause-and-consequence analysis
4. Synthesizing a causal loop diagram

Detailing Functional Activities. During this exercise, the facilitators distributed quantities of 3"-by-5" cards to the team members. They asked each team member to think of all the tasks involved in selling and delivering electrical power to CPP's customers, and to write one task on each card. Next, the team grouped their various cards under function headings posted on the wall. Finally, the participants broke into 10 sub-teams, each of which took responsibility for further affinitizing function groupings. This task resulted in activity subgroups under each function, as well as needed inputs to the function, the sources of those inputs, outputs from the function, and the destinations of those outputs (see "A Sales Function Example"). As a final step, the teams labeled activities they thought were done well and those they thought were problematic.

Analyzing Functional Relationships. Now each function team analyzed how the inputs and outputs from their function linked up with inputs and outputs of other CPP functions or with outside entities such as customers, regulatory agencies, and so forth. In the resulting diagonal matrix, the functions were placed on a diagonal from top left to bottom right (see "A Functional Relationship Matrix" on p. 28). The functions' outputs were placed to either side, and inputs appeared above and below the functions. For example, in the illustration, items 1 and 2—filled-out order forms and customer complaint records—are outputs of the "Sales" function. Item 2 is also an input to the "Marketing" function. Item 3 is an input to the "Sales" function as well as an output from "Marketing." Finally, the team again labeled problem areas and areas where work was done well.

Assembling the matrix gave the participants a holistic view of how work was actually accomplished at CPP, and generated intense interest and energy. One 25-year CPP veteran exclaimed that this was the first time he had seen how "the whole thing came together." The matrix also helped participants identify major problem areas, both internal and external.

A SALES FUNCTION EXAMPLE

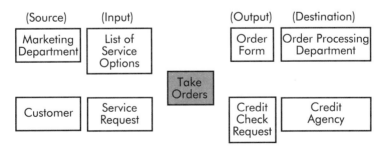

To perform the subgroup activity of taking orders, the CPP staff member needs several kinds of inputs. For example, he or she needs a list of the company's service options, which comes from the marketing department. The output of an order—a filled-out order form—then goes to the order processing department.

A FUNCTIONAL RELATIONSHIP MATRIX

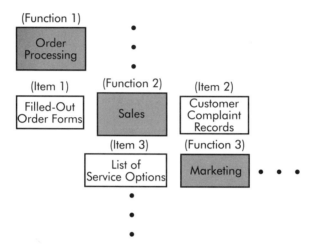

This is an excerpt from CPP's larger matrix. In a diagonal matrix, outputs appear to either side of the functions, and inputs are above and below. With this kind of diagram, you can graphically depict the mapping between any number of functions.

Performing a Root-Cause-and-Consequence Analysis. The teams next used fishbone diagramming techniques (a commonly used quality improvement tool) to focus on the causes and consequences of the problem areas they had identified earlier. They copied each problem, as well as each area of competency, onto individual cards. They then sorted the many cards into "like" groupings, or clusters, and named them, with the goal being to identify root causes and major consequences of each cluster (see "A Root-Cause-and-Consequence Diagram").

This process helped make the number of problematic areas less overwhelming. It also gave the teams a new understanding of both the underlying reasons for their problems and the true costs to CPP of those problems, and suggested a series of key variables at work in the organization's dynamics. Based on this foundation of insights about cause and effect, the group moved in a natural manner to the next stage: creating a causal loop diagram.

Synthesizing a Causal Loop Diagram. As the teams filled out their cause-and-consequences charts, they began to see that the consequence of one analysis often turned out to be the root cause of another. For example,

A ROOT-CAUSE-AND-CONSEQUENCE DIAGRAM

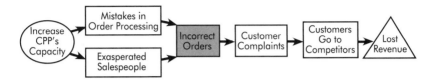

This diagram is a simplification of one part of CPP's larger diagram. In this section, the problem cluster—customer complaints—is in a rectangle at the center. The rectangles to the left are possible root causes of the problem, and the oval to the far left contains an idea for remedying the problem. The rectangles to the right of the problem cluster are consequences of the problem, and the triangle to the far right represents a measurable outcome of the problem (in this case, loss of revenue).

the group realized that the more revenue was lost, the harder it was for CPP to beef up their capacity to service new business. The complex, dynamic nature of these connections soon became apparent, and the team realized that they needed a new way to represent the connections and the feedback patterns that they exhibited.

The group took the work "offline" and began using pieces of twine to show the various linkages among key variables. It's important to note that the creation of a causal loop diagram was neither an implicit nor an explicit goal of the work at this time. In a sense, the group "backed into" the process of diagramming feedback loops by noticing connections during the earlier exercises, and by realizing that they needed a different way to represent them so as to understand more deeply how things worked at CPP.

With the aid of the commissioner, the group synthesized the final form of their causal loop diagram. The diagram evolved through the telling of stories about the various connections and feedback loops. Through these stories, team members dropped some variables, added others, and began identifying what turned out to be reinforcing and balancing processes.

"A Glimpse at CPP's Causal Loop Diagram" on p. 30 shows just a portion of the final representation. This particular piece focuses on the dynamic problems that began plaguing CPP after it launched its bond-funded growth effort. The diagram resembles a "Limits to Success"

A GLIMPSE AT CPP'S CAUSAL LOOP DIAGRAM

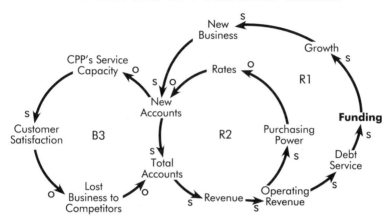

CPP's growth efforts, fueled by bond funding, led to more business than the company could handle. As CPP began struggling to service its rapidly rising number of new accounts, customers grumbled and competitors began stealing business from CPP. CPP's total accounts declined, which put a limit on the original growth engines.

archetypal situation, with two growth engines (R1 and R2) and a balancing loop that slows the growth as the company hits its capacity limits (B3). The first growth engine began with the bond-issue funding, which inspired CPP to expand. The company's growth effort generated new business, increasing the number of new accounts. As total accounts increased, rising revenues allowed higher operating revenue, which let CPP service its debt, which led to increased funding. As a second growth engine, rising revenues increased CPP's purchasing power, which allowed the company to lower rates and thereby encourage yet additional new accounts. However, all this new business ran up against a key limit: CPP's ability to service the rapidly rising number of accounts (B3). As this ability declined, so did customer satisfaction. Competitors began grabbing some of those dissatisfied customers, which reduced CPP's total accounts and put a limit on the amount of growth generated by R1 and R2.

The Value of Causal Mapping

The process that CPP used to eventually arrive at their causal loop diagram has several benefits that are worth noting here. First, creating the diagram without using explicit modeling methods—i.e., by "backing into" the loops instead—lets people develop a sense of feedback processes without getting distracted or overwhelmed by what may seem like formal causal loop terminology and concepts. For many people, this process therefore leads to a more natural deepening of their understanding. Second, this method is far less intimidating for people who tend to want to "get it right" when they first start trying to draw causal loop diagrams. Arriving at a diagram "from the ground up" can lead to a stronger sense of ownership on the part of the people who constructed it—a vital quality if a change effort is to be sustained. Finally—and most important—the process brought to light all the realities that stemmed from the functional relationships at CPP. Because the participants in this series of exercises were not managers but the actual people who performed the work in their various functions, the process captured how work really happened at the company. For CPP, this richness, along with the earlier exercises, proved key to ensuring lasting, large-scale change. ⌐

RESULTS OF CPP'S CHANGE EFFORT

CPP's analysis of current reality and the transformation action plan that it designed based on the insights it gained from this series of exercises led to dramatic results. The company made an impressive turnaround and has been enjoying a new degree of financial health. Specifically, CPP's revenues increased by 26 percent over the period 1995 and 1996, while its operation and maintenance expenses increased by only 3.4 percent. Also, in 1996, revenue per CPP account increased by 15 percent compared to 1994, before the redesign effort started, reflecting a more efficient capital utilization. The end result was that 1996 marked by far the most impressive financial performance for CPP in the 1990s.

Equally significant, CPP's improved financial and management position was recognized by Wall Street when, in December 1996, Moody's upgraded CPP's rating to a long-term "A" at a time when most public utilities were going through downgrading. Moody's upgrade of CPP's rating confirmed the strength of CPP's financial position. According to Moody's, CPP earned this rating by demonstrating a strong competitive position to meet the restructuring of the electric industry, a refocused expansion and marketing plan, a proactive management effort to meet the challenges of the existing competitive environment, and an established record of satisfying margins through managing operating expenses.

Nagah Ramadan is the executive vice president of RCC Consultants, Inc. He served as commissioner for the Cleveland Department of Public Utilities from 1994 to 1997, during the transformation effort described in this article.

Patrick Parker-Roach is a vice president in the Enterprise Customer Management practice of Technology Solutions Company. He has 23 years of experience in business process reengineering, business development management, and other technical and organizational fields.

Chapter Four

The Organizational Learning Goal at Ford's EFHD

by David Berdish

Electrical and Fuel Handling (EFHD), the smallest division at Ford Motor Company, employed about 7,000 people in the early 1990s and did approximately $1.5 billion in sales annually. We manufactured starters, alternators, injectors, ignition coils—everything that sparks and gasses your car. In those years, we faced tremendous challenges in terms of our global competitiveness, some of which had to do with our unique relationship to Ford Motor Company.

Even though EFHD was a division of Ford, the program managers at Ford were not obligated to purchase our parts—they were free to buy from our Japanese and German competitors. And yet, we were affected by Ford's policies and practices in ways that made it difficult for us to compete against those foreign suppliers. For example, we needed to invest in best-in-class technology and a high-powered engineering corps, but as part of the Ford 2000 restructuring program, we were expected to reduce our engineering resources. We also needed to stay cost competitive, but because of our union workforce, we had a high wage rate relative to our competitors.

The Ford 2000 program also pushed us to become global. In the early 1990s, we launched plants in Northern Ireland and Hungary, and engineering centers in Michigan, England, Germany, and Japan. We then opened plants in Brazil and Mexico and received direction to launch plants in the Far East. In order to meet these challenges, we knew we needed to operate in entirely new ways. That's why, in 1992, we made the goal of becoming a learning organization part of our strategic initiative.

Knowledge vs. Understanding

Our organizational learning efforts focused on enhancing our tactical knowledge with a better understanding of the larger systems. For example, we were very good at analyzing processes that were out of control; however, a process that was completely in control might not necessarily be functioning optimally. So, in addition to working on root causes, we needed to tackle common cause issues. And while we were analyzing, we also needed to synthesize, to understand the interrelationships in the system. We needed to augment our accounting methods and fishbone diagrams with hexagons and causal loops. And in addition to knowing how to discuss, we wanted to be able to dialogue. Through this synthesis of traditional methods with organizational learning tools, we hoped to leverage our process knowledge with a level of systems understanding that would lead to quantum improvements.

Deployment: Five Areas

To embed the learning organization approach within EFHD, we worked simultaneously in five areas: culture, awareness, capacity, involvement, and community.

Culture. In order to create a work environment in which people felt empowered to learn, we needed to build a culture based on trust and openness so people could feel comfortable taking risks. We wanted to encourage people to share best practices and discourage competition between plants or product teams.

Awareness. Building awareness of our activities across teams included communications methods such as email, as well as documentation of our work and the lessons learned. It also involved internal facilitation. We assembled a staff of seven people who facilitated team learning projects and communicated the learning initiatives across the division. These facilitators were supported by outside people, such as MIT researchers and faculty from our local Washtenaw Community College.

Capacity. In order to strengthen our internal capacity, we developed a learning course in partnership with our local community college. In this intensive, week-long course, people from our Michigan and Indiana plants came together with employees from our overseas divisions to learn the basic theory and skills of the learning organization. They also worked through concrete examples of how we applied systems thinking and team learning at EFHD.

Involvement. All of the involvement in organizational learning at our division was done through invitation, not by mandate. We believed that this type of change simply couldn't be forced upon people. People who *did* want to get involved could do so through the learning organization course, through our Total Productive Maintenance workshops (which incorporated an organizational learning approach), or by participating in learning teams. Upper management was also involved in the efforts. Our top 16 executives took the MIT core competency course together, and participated in a weekly two-hour dialogue in which they worked on their own team issues and provided a leadership example for the whole division.

Community. As another focus of our work, we built a learning community by cultivating relationships inside Ford, with participants from the MIT Learning Center (now the Society for Organizational Learning), and in the Washtenaw community. By nurturing these relationships, we felt we could maximize our learning from all opportunities, and also become good corporate citizens both inside and outside of Ford.

To implement these five objectives, we concentrated on three activities: the introductory course, dialogue circles, and learning teams.

Introductory Course

In the mid-1990s, we conducted an introductory class with the local community college on systems thinking and organizational learning. In this course, participants learned the basic concepts of organizational learning and gained hands-on experience with tools such as systems

---

MULTIPLE APPROACHES

Culture:	Provide a culture based on trust, honesty, and openness.
Awareness:	Increase awareness of organizational learning by developing communications and media that are available to all employees.
Capacity Building:	Provide resources and capacity to meet employees' demands for learning courses, projects, facilitation, and documentation.
Involvement:	Increase involvement of all employees in learning projects to create maximum performance in manufacturing operations, customer relations, and shared vision.
Community:	Build relationships with other organizations and learn "state-of-the-art" methods and tools.

archetypes and dialogue. The course was taught by a professor from the college, who provided the conceptual and theoretical framework, and an EFHD facilitator, who helped participants apply those tools to real business issues. We eventually ran six courses per year in our Michigan facility, and hosted three courses in our overseas plant by the end of 1996.

Classes consisted of about 50 people, and we tried to balance attendance between hourly and salaried workers, and local and overseas employees. As part of our community-building efforts, we also invited spouses of Ford employees, as well as people from local universities, city government, the community college, and other companies. This gave us a diversity of perspectives, which we found invaluable.

Our Division Operating Committee also participated in each course by joining us for some of the group presentations around culture and visioning. They also took part in a dialogue so that attendees could experience a

---

"You're not a learning organization because you know how to dialogue. You're a learning organization when you know how to turn dialogue into decision."

---

dialogue session conducted by people familiar with the process. Finally, they joined us for the opening reception and participated in the celebration dinner and graduation ceremony.

Dialogue Circles

Strategic dialogue became one of the most useful tools for team learning and effective problem-solving at EFHD. In part, this was because it provided an opportunity to think about issues and problems on a different level. As teams practiced dialogue, they created an infrastructure for more open, honest communication.

Teams throughout the division used dialogue on an ongoing basis, and the practice became global. When the Division Operating Committee members visited overseas plants, they sat in a circle and talked for a day. No books. No reviews. No measurements. Just an open conversation about the issues facing the plant and how they might do things differently. When you have a plant located in a place like Belfast, Northern Ireland, there's a lot going on besides producing parts. We believed the dialogue approach provided a broader perspective on the issues and helped us tackle them more effectively.

In the weekly dialogue, the Division Operating Committee's one ground rule was that committee members didn't necessarily have to tackle specific problems, nor were they required to come out of the sessions with solutions. But they very often *would* talk about specific issues and come to a much better understanding of the problems, which led to more effective solutions.

The fact that there were no "hard" measurements in a dialogue session does not mean that this process lacked hard results. Peter Senge once said, "You're not a learning organization because you know how to

---

The surfacing of mental models and assumptions helped pave the way for honest communication and a more effective approach to problems.

---

dialogue. You're a learning organization when you know how to turn dialogue into decision." In our dialogues, there was no such thing as taking notes or trying to transcribe the conversation. But, if we did hit an "aha," we stopped, had the team leader write down the insight or action item, and assigned it to someone. Attaching accountability and responsibility to our processes played a key role in all of our learning organization work.

One of the best examples of the "hard" results that can come from this process emerged from a dialogue among members of the product launch success team. At one point in the dialogue an engineering manager asked, "Why is it that the machines always seem to work fine on Saturday?" The assumption behind his statement was that union workers were pleased when machines broke down Monday through Friday, because they could get two hours' overtime to fix them. If a machine broke down on Friday, that was even better, because the workers got all day Saturday to fix it. However, by 3:30 on Saturday afternoon they wanted to go home and spend the weekend with their families, so the machines didn't break down.

A UAW representative immediately took offense to the remark. "I'm sick of you guys implying that the UAW sabotages the machines. It's my opinion the machines don't work at EFHD because you have young engineers buying these machines, and all they do is buy crap."

At that point, someone from purchasing joined in. "You know, I buy the same darn machines for seven other divisions at Ford, and they seem to work fine everywhere else. I think you guys have trouble with equipment because you have terrible Total Productive Maintenance procedures."

This was not a pleasant exchange, but the surfacing of mental models and assumptions helped pave the way for honest communication and a more effective approach to the problems that were raised. In order to address the issue of machine breakdowns, the group developed an equipment specifications manual that covered all aspects of testing and installing new machinery. This manual proved so effective that it served as the prototype for the whole company. When they looked into the supplier/purchasing issue further, the team discovered that some suppliers were, in fact, taking advantage of EFHD's young engineers. They were selling us six or seven spare parts for machines when only one would break down in an entire lifetime. The team subsequently developed a consignment policy that required suppliers to keep the spare parts in their inventory. That step alone saved us hundreds of thousands of dollars in inventory costs.

Learning Teams

Most of the activities that took place around organizational learning at EFHD occurred in "learning teams." These were cross-functional groups of people who applied organizational learning tools to their jobs and processes in order to become more effective. Learning teams were an important part of our organizational learning activities, because they provided an infrastructure for approaching problems from multiple perspectives. In fact, we found that our most successful learning efforts were the ones that contained the most cross-functional diversity.

Most learning team projects followed a similar process. The teams began by generating issues to be studied—usually during dialogue sessions or through the use of graphical facilitation techniques (such as hexagons). Then the teams used causal loop diagrams and systems archetypes to look at the critical core issues that surfaced. They also incorporated visioning and talked about their desired outcomes—for our processes, but also for the future of EFHD. Once they felt they had a good understanding of both the problem and the desired outcome, they went into action and figured out what tools would be most effective—TPM, value management, total cost management, kaizen, etc. Throughout this process, the team spent a lot of time in reflection, particularly through ongoing dialogue, which generated more issues and led to more action. This became a continuous improvement loop.

The first learning team that we formed was the product launch success team. This seemed an appropriate place to start, since traditional business tools such as root-cause analysis had been inadequate for the

---

REWARD AND RECOGNITION

In order to deeply embed organizational learning in our infrastructure, we have paid particular attention to our reward and recognition practices. One of the challenges we had to overcome was our tendency to reward results over improvement efforts. If product managers are promoted based solely on the success or failure of their launch, they will be less open to sharing their most successful strategies (for fear of losing their "competitive edge" over other managers) and less willing to share their failures (for fear of "looking bad"), both of which decrease the learning opportunities for the division as a whole.

To overcome this tendency, we have tried hard to reward commitment to organizational learning. In the last three years, the program managers that have been the most honest and most open with their learning—both in terms of things gone right and things gone wrong—have been promoted. In one of those cases, the launch was less successful in terms of the hard metrics, but the manager did a wonderful job of making sure that all current and future managers knew what went well and what didn't. When these promotions were announced, the message was clear: These people were recognized not only for launching their products successfully, but also for supporting organizational learning throughout EFHD.

Learning is now seen as a critical metric for whether people exhibit the leadership styles necessary to be part of top management at EFHD.

type of process redesign we wanted. As part of our product launch project, any group that had completed a launch was required to share its experiences with people who were launching products in the current year. We incorporated this practice into the process of "handing over the baton." After this, any new product launch team had access to the lessons provided by program managers from 1992 to 1995.

We started the learning team concept in 1992. By the end of that year, we had two teams involving a total of 32 people. In 1993, the numbers jumped to seven teams, 120 people. In 1994, they hit 20 teams, about 500 people. In 1996, we had 32 teams and 1200 people involved in the team learning projects, totaling 20 percent of our workforce. Each team was organized around a particular goal or objective. The product launch teams, for example, continually worked to improve our quality, cost, and timeliness on new products. We had 21 product teams that focused on removing costs from our products. Other teams included QOS (quality operating systems), scheduling, customer relations, capacity planning, and total productive maintenance.

Results

We feel that the results of our organizational learning work speak for themselves. Our earnings increased significantly through the mid-1990s. Our launch costs, timing, and technology improved every year since 1992. Our quality metrics increased by double-digit percentages, and we saved millions of dollars in warranty costs. In 1995 we cut 50 percent out of our product launch budget. We reduced our response time to material cost changes from 89 weeks to about 60 weeks, which yielded significant savings. We built full-service technology and design responsibility in house, and our product launches became so smooth that it was almost impossible to tell that we were going through them. Our division led all the divisions of Ford Motor Company in its achievement of Total Productive Maintenance checkpoints.

On the people side, our surveys revealed that employees noticed a positive change in our culture. They felt less stressed and more empowered than before. All of our management team—especially our general manager, who reported on our progress to the executive committee at Ford—were willing to say those results were associated with our organizational learning activities.

Next Steps

As we looked to the late 1990s, our future plans were twofold: (1) deepening the level of understanding among people who were already involved in organizational learning projects; and (2) spreading the awareness of organizational learning more broadly throughout EFHD. To deepen the learning, we talked about designing an advanced course for people who wanted to gain more expertise in the organizational learning tools, and we considered adding computer modeling to our approach.

As for increasing awareness throughout EFHD, we still had a long way to go in taking the organizational learning practices to our overseas plants. The challenge we faced there was how we could learn together as a global organization when the people involved not only had different viewpoints, but also different cultures and worldviews. For example, in the U.S. we talked a lot about "fear of management." But the people in our plant in Hungary—who had grown up under a communist regime— had pointed out that the American definition of fear is very different from theirs! Surfacing such mental models becomes even more of a challenge when you were speaking across different languages. We needed to find ways to transcend the linguistic and cultural barriers that existed and make the concepts of organizational learning accessible to everyone.

Learning and Survival

The tremendous impact that organizational learning had at EFHD was apparent in both our improvement in metrics and the increased involvement and initiative of our employees. At one week-long program, an hourly worker said, "For years and years, not only the mental model but the reality at EFHD was that employees were used strictly for their physical abilities. It's really a pleasure that now we're being asked to use our minds."

In 1991, the Big Three auto manufacturers were convinced they did not need to have their component suppliers be part of their company. Chrysler got rid of most of theirs. GM set up many of its component suppliers as subsidiaries. But EFHD became living proof that organizational learning really does work.

Epilogue

In 1997, Ford's Electrical and Fuel Handling Division became part of Visteon Automotive Systems. When Visteon ($18 billion in sales and

85,000 employees, 80 plants, and 30 engineering centers in 19 countries) was born in September 1997, it embarked on a quest to become a high-performing enterprise and learning community. The 1992–1996 learning efforts of EFHD provided leadership and lessons for the new journey when Bob Womac was named Visteon Executive Vice-President of Automotive Operations and David Berdish was named Process Leadership/Learning Organization Manager.

At Visteon, the same core requirements for creating a learning organization exist as did for the EFHD. These include the development of a robust infrastructure; the time commitment for dialogue; the sponsorship of learning teams; the importance of learning in the Visteon values and behaviors; the approval of a learning course; and the endorsement of a chief executive who believes strongly and completely in the effort.

However, no one closely involved in the effort ever anticipated the complexity of scale that would arise at Visteon. The challenges include arriving at a collective understanding of the enterprise's view; developing a systems-focused business; managing Visteon's incredible cultural, regional, and functional diversity; and honing our ability to manage seven individual business—each of which believes it runs better than the other six. The Visteon learning team has had to exhibit motivation, passion, and a thick skin, and has had to be quite sensitive to "learning space" and the delivery of the message. As the team continues to develop its understanding of the complexity involved, hones its perspective, and screws up its courage, then Visteon will seize the possibilities and become one of the finest organizations in the world. ◄

David Berdish is the process leadership/learning organization manager at Visteon, an enterprise of Ford Motor Company. He has been with Ford since 1983, including six years as the process leadership manager at the Electrical and Fuel Handling Division, where he led the Learning Organization strategic initiative. David earned a B.A. from the University of Michigan and an M.S. from Virginia Commonwealth University. He is on the Executive Council of the Society for Organizational Learning and is a board member of the Washtenaw Education-Work Consortium.

ABC: Initiating Large-Scale Change at Chrysler

by Dave Meador

When Chrysler adopted activity-based costing (ABC) in 1991, the decision represented more than a simple accounting change. The shift to ABC challenged many of our previous assumptions about cost and profitability, as well as our operating procedures (see "Activity-Based Costing" on p. 44). For example, an automobile part that might have been calculated to cost $100 under the old cost system could cost $3,000 under the new one, and vice versa. To product line managers or other executives whose profits and overall performance are tied to these numbers, ABC presented a huge threat.

In addition, converting to ABC can be quite intrusive. Tracking activity-based costs requires a thorough understanding of the processes that go into making each car. Thus, setting up an ABC method means interviewing and surveying people throughout a plant to find out what work they do and how they do it. Because of the challenges and threats posed by ABC, it has experienced a 70 percent failure rate in companies across the U.S. At Chrysler, our finance staff knew that in order to make ABC work, we needed to do more than just communicate its nuts-and-bolts; we had to establish a process for handling the changes in assumptions and operations that the conversion required.

Early Warning Signs: Resistance from Within

We vastly underestimated the potential resistance to ABC throughout the company. The finance people who joined the ABC team thought they were embarking on a leading-edge project, but as the resistance to ABC

ACTIVITY-BASED COSTING

Activity-based costing (ABC) is a relatively new approach to cost accounting that tracks costs according to the processes and activities that go into making a product. Unlike traditional cost-accounting methods, which allocate overhead according to such factors as labor costs, ABC calculates these costs according to the resources each product requires. This method provides a better understanding of the actual production costs and leads to more informed manufacturing and corporate-wide strategic decisions than traditional accounting methods.

---

compounded throughout the company, they began to question their career move. Stress and fear of failure ran high among team members, and some of us considered recommending that management abandon the project.

About that time, we started working with Fred Kofman at the former MIT Center for Organizational Learning. Because Fred's background was in accounting, we thought he might be able to help us identify the roots of the resistance. After talking to people throughout the company, Fred concluded that it wasn't the plant managers' resistance that was hindering the ABC effort—it was actually the finance team's way of working with these managers. We were asking people to think in dramatically different ways about how they ran their business, but how willing were we to consider new ways of doing our work?

With Fred's help, we realized that large-scale change such as the kind we were proposing had to begin with each of us on the finance team. We needed to model new ways of working together and thinking about change if we were to expect the same of others. By practicing the tools and disciplines of organizational learning, we hoped not only to improve our ability to function as a team, but also to enhance our effectiveness in implementing ABC throughout the company.

The Tools of Organizational Learning

Since many of the ABC team members were finance MBAs who were now spending most of their time serving as teachers and coaches, we knew they needed support and practice in learning new skills. With Fred's help, we designed several workshops on organizational learning to develop our skills in areas such as systems thinking, effective conversations, dialogue, and stress management.

Each two- to three-day workshop focused on specific tools or techniques of organizational learning. We asked people to come to the sessions prepared with actual case studies. For example, if several people had just experienced a difficult conversation or meeting, the group might focus on improving their conversational skills (suspending assumptions, using the "left-hand column" exercise, balancing inquiry and advocacy, etc.). If we felt that people needed a stronger grounding in how to think in terms of interconnections and unintended consequences, we might focus on the tools of systems thinking. In addition to these focused work sessions, we held seminars every few months on stress management, to help people handle the demands being placed on them. This included teaching them reflection tools such as journaling and meditation.

We also worked extensively on the disciplines of personal mastery and dialogue to build our internal team. We held some Outward Bound–type sessions and created practice fields for role-playing tough conversations. For example, if I were anticipating a difficult conversation with a plant manager, and I wanted to practice that dialogue with a colleague, we would run through the scenario with one of us first playing the part of the plant manager. Then we'd switch. Role-playing let us practice what we wanted to say in a nonthreatening setting, and helped us appreciate both sides of the issue.

The Implementation Process

After spending some time developing our own skills, we began using the tools of organizational learning to redesign how we implemented ABC in the company. In partnership with our external consultants (who also received organizational learning training), we reevaluated how we were engaging our "clients" in launching our projects.

Traditionally, we would arrive at a plant, sit down with the plant manager, and say, "We know you're really busy—your operations are running seven days a week, twenty-four hours a day—so we don't want to bother you. We'll just go ahead and change your cost and reporting systems for you, and here's how we'll do it."

Six months later, however, we might discover that the plant manager didn't understand the leadership role he or she had to play in supporting the change, didn't feel committed to the project, and didn't understand how to use the new information—all of which led to problems in applying ABC throughout the plant. We knew we needed to change our approach, but we didn't think the plant managers would commit to the time we needed up front. Our mental model was, "They're too busy, they're not going to be interested, let's not even ask."

So we practiced making requests properly. We learned how to sit down with the plant managers and say, "Listen, if we're going to do this right, we need three full days of your time and your plant management team's time." This type of request was unheard of—plant management teams never went off site for one day, let alone three. But after practicing the conversation, we went out and asked, and much to our surprise, all of the teams agreed to give us the time we needed.

"Flying" ABC

Once we had tackled the initial engagement process, we turned to improving how we communicated the benefits of ABC. Rather than use a traditional overhead slide presentation to "convince" the managers of the need for an activity-based costing system, we developed a management "flight simulator." With this tool, plant managers could experience for themselves the operational consequences of the old finance system versus the

---

The simulator was a great way to introduce plant managers to the concept of systems thinking. It encouraged a new way of learning, by getting people engaged in an interactive tool.

ABC approach. Much to their surprise, the managers discovered that, because of the way overhead costs are allocated in the different cost systems, the old approach might lead them to continue investing in unprofitable product lines, or to underinvest in profitable ones.

The simulator was also a great way to introduce plant managers to the concept of systems thinking. Moreover, it encouraged a new way of learning, by getting people engaged in an interactive tool for understanding the advantages of ABC. In some cases, we went one step further and created a simulated microworld of a portion of their plant. This involved process mapping and costing a key operation to teach them about ABC using their data, not a textbook case or another Chrysler plant. Providing relevant information worked well in breaking down defensive posturing. So although the creation of individual microworlds was time consuming, the investment paid off.

In order to support the ongoing work of ABC, we created several additional seminars that were scheduled throughout the conversion process. For example, the "midstream" seminar, which was timed to coincide with the release of the first ABC-based reports, addressed the fear and anxiety people might feel when deluged with new information. At this point, we emphasized that the objective was to provide measurement for *learning* (as part of a Plan-Do-Check-Act process), versus measurement for *reporting*.

Finally, a transition seminar was held at the end of the project to deal with issues of ongoing commitment. This session was particularly valuable because in many cases of ABC implementation failures, we found that the breakdown occurred not because someone committed to an action and then didn't follow through, but because the "conditions of satisfaction" for the request had not been clearly articulated and agreed upon up front.

In none of these seminars did we focus explicitly on "teaching people about organizational learning." Instead, we simply used the tools of organizational learning as part of our everyday activities. For example, at the start of a workshop or meeting we would have a "check-in," where we would go around the room and ask everyone to say what they are bringing with them to this meeting. Many people had never taken part in a check-in, so it signaled a very different way of acting with people. It is worth noting that we did not use the term "check-in" to describe this process, and in general we learned not to use organizational learning jargon. In our experience, the use of such terms actually increased resistance, and was unnecessary.

Management Involvement and Commitment

A critical success factor for this project was the active involvement of senior managers and their role as a support network. Bob Lutz, the president of Chrysler, was a major spokesperson for the effort. He also created an environment that enabled the ABC team to productively share our concerns and beliefs. For example, at one point there was a very frank conversation about the need to slow down the project in order to allow time for the cultural changes that were necessary.

Jim Donlon, the corporate controller, and Gary Valade, the CFO, were actively involved in both the technical and cultural side of this effort. Their contributions included everything from persistently using the ABC approach in a variety of corporate decisions to learning and practicing many of the tools of organizational learning.

From Failure to Success

As a result of our work in organizational learning and team building, there was a dramatic change in the acceptance of ABC throughout Chrysler. Among the finance team, the difference could almost be felt in the shift in energy and stress levels. Pushing people around and trying to force change on them is an exhausting process, whereas listening to people and working with them on change is energizing. After some early successes, in which ABC data was used for cost reductions or investment proposals, plant managers began seeking us out to help them implement the new system.

The last thing we learned from ABC is that the rate of organizational change is limited by the rate of personal change—not by the rate at which we can introduce new technology.

Over time, people started to notice that the ABC group's failures seemed to be turning into successes, and our work gained wider attention throughout Chrysler. Members of the ABC team appeared more relaxed than before, and they were no longer trying to tunnel their way out of the department. Outside people even expressed interest in joining the group, and their enthusiasm generated further excitement. As people noticed these changes, they began asking if they could attend our seminars. Based on the acceptance of ABC at Chrysler, we started redesigning our financial systems to fully embed ABC principles throughout the costing systems.

Eventually, Chrysler decided that it would sponsor its own internal five-day Core Competency Course (based on the course offered by the former MIT Center for Organizational Learning). By fall 1996, more than 600 people had attended the program, and many have begun applying the tools to their everyday work. An organizational learning approach is now being used in other large-scale change initiatives at Chrysler, including manufacturing and engineering.

Lessons Learned

In our experience with ABC, we learned that organizational transformation starts with personal transformation. We had to stop focusing solely on why the system is so dysfunctional ("What's wrong? Who goofed up?") and begin looking at how we each contribute to that dysfunction.

We also learned that change agents require a support network. Before the ABC initiative, we would typically take some bright person from a leading university, put that person in a plant and say, "OK, go ahead and make things different." After about six months, that person would burn out because there would be nobody to help, to offer support, or to share experiences. It was just the individual against the system.

We found that, in addition to providing them with a support network, the change agents themselves can benefit from improving the way they make requests, offers, and promises. This helps create an environment in which people can feel more comfortable asking for help or offering assistance.

The last thing we learned from ABC, a lesson that is hard to swallow, is that the rate of organizational change is limited by the rate of personal change—not by the rate at which we can introduce new technology. Putting new information systems on the floor, incorporating a new technology into a plant, or designing a new product is a fairly straightforward process. It is how fast you can transform people that will govern how fast you can change the system in which they are operating.

The ABC initiative became a five-year journey for us. One thing that we all came to realize is that patience is essential when you're facing large-scale change. It takes us decades to form the mental models we have today, and we can't expect them to change in one four-hour class. This work is really about deep-seated change, and that sort of effort takes time.

Dave Meador was manager of financial and performance measures at Chrysler Corporation, which involved redesigning many of Chrysler's financial systems and implementing new performance measures. He is now vice president and controller at DTE Energy.

Part Two

Addressing Critical Business Challenges

In Part I, we saw examples of large-scale change initiatives. In Part II, we get a close look at highly focused, deep change: companies that used the tools and principles of organizational learning to address a specific, pressing business challenge. In some cases—for example, Ford's manufacturing reengineering program and the U.S. Navy's redesign of its acquisitions team—the organization involved sought to reevaluate its operating strategies. In other cases, such as Kellogg Brown & Root's new approach to project debriefing, the company set out to improve its team learning capacity in a localized setting. In yet other cases, these organizations strove to reduce expenses while improving customer service, to address new global challenges, or to ease the way to introducing a new technology.

The stories in Part II open a window onto the nature of deep, focused change within an organizational context. As in Part I, the selection is richly varied, featuring accounts from industry, from education, and from healthcare. The broad array of settings reveals the unique challenges faced by each kind of organization, and the universal struggles and successes experienced by all of them.

Manufacturing Reengineering at Ford: A Flexible Strategy for Introducing Organizational Learning

by Ann-Marie Krul and Don Mroz

From 1995 to 1997, the Ford Process Leadership Office's Organizational Learning Team introduced organizational learning as a facilitation tool for major reengineering projects, based on a dynamic, adaptable strategy. We used the work of Margaret Wheatley (self-organizing systems) and Dee Hock (chaordic organizations) as a foundation for this approach, which involved creating a safe environment for experimentation and learning.

To gain credibility, we sought to leverage existing practices that we thought fit well with organizational learning principles. We also linked our efforts to important, real-life business challenges. In addition, we avoided "selling" the five disciplines (as defined by Peter Senge in *The Fifth Discipline*) to employees, but rather invited people to participate in the learning process and provided assistance to those who requested it. In the end, many employees did not see our efforts as an explicit "strategy" for introducing organizational learning—which helped us gain greater acceptance for these concepts and tools.

In this chapter, we share an approach for introducing and using organizational learning principles, tools, and methodologies that has produced positive results for Ford Motor Company. We hope that others will experiment with our learnings, add to them, try different approaches, and build new strategies that work for their organizations.

Background

Ford Motor Company's experience with organizational learning began in the late 1980s, with Peter Senge's and Russ Ackoff's participation in a senior executive training program. Some executives then took the work to the next level, integrating organizational learning concepts and tools in their business units. Pockets of practice formed in different areas of the company around these leaders.

During the next few years, numerous employees participated in the MIT core course in organizational learning and in other training offered within Ford. Application of the material ranged from small team efforts, to a vehicle program team involving hundreds of people, to a divisional venture comprising several thousand workers. The Electrical and Fuel Handling Division (EFHD) undertook one of the most successful and sustained organizational learning projects (see Chapter 4). By the mid 1990s, groups of practitioners and leaders were applying learning theories, methods, and tools to realize business goals. For instance, Visteon Automotive Systems, an enterprise of Ford Motor Company, is now applying many of the lessons learned during the EFHD project.

Launching the Manufacturing Project

With the inception of Ford 2000—a corporate initiative to make Ford the leading automotive company in the world—the Process Leadership Office was formed to take an enterprise-wide view of the business and help transform its major processes. In late 1995, Process Leadership appointed an Organizational Learning (OL) Team to apply these concepts to major reengineering projects, focusing first on manufacturing. Managers in this area believed that organizational learning could enable plants to implement new production techniques and create effective work groups by practicing methods and tools that fostered open and honest communication.

The OL Team consisted of four people and had strong, visible sponsorship from the vice president of Process Leadership. This support was key in legitimizing organizational learning throughout Ford. We also had substantial resources in the form of seed money to help groups implement organizational learning; executive support from leaders throughout the company; access to the Organizational Learning Center at MIT (now the Society for Organizational Learning); interaction with local academic institutions; and a powerful network of external and internal practitioners and capacity builders.

A key part of our approach was building capacity through partnerships—some formal, others quite informal—with universities, community colleges, and external consultants. These relationships provided a forum for experimenting with curriculum offerings and new ways to deliver organizational learning material. We consciously linked research, capacity building, and application, following the model developed by the Society for Organizational Learning.

The Formal-Informal Strategy

We began our work by expanding the OL Team to include the organizational learning managers from Human Resources and the Electrical and Fuel Handling Division. We then created the following strategy:

- Implement a "formal-informal" approach to support interested individuals and groups—informal in that we sought to pull in those who were predisposed to this kind of work, and formal in that we then provided them with tools and training.

- Seek opportunities to engage the manufacturing leadership, reengineering team, and plants in creating a shared understanding and coordinated plan to implement the reengineering project. Foster genuine commitment by co-creating the learning effort with managers.

- Focus on the systemic understanding of the manufacturing reengineering project (that is, the "why" and high-level "what's") to complement the comprehensive reengineering training (the "how's").

- Ground the learning effort in explicit business goals.

- Don't "sell" the organizational learning initiative; rather, let people make an informed choice about participating in the effort. Avoid becoming "another corporate initiative"; go for commitment rather than mere compliance.

- Use the five disciplines as a common language and framework for teams to enhance their effectiveness.

- Leverage external expertise to provide strong support to teams, achieve quick successes, and build internal capacity. Identify people who can become internal coaches to sustain the effort beyond its initial phase.

Working with the Plants

With a strategy in place, the OL Team chose six plants to partner with initially. Two additional plants that had previously started learning efforts on their own became part of our developing network, serving as a resource for the other plants.

We began our work with the plants by designing "learning labs"—interactive workshops that focused on the plants' business goals. We also partnered with an outside firm to develop a system dynamics simulation to help plant managers and their management teams gain a systemic understanding of the manufacturing reengineering project. This learning tool showed how systems thinking principles could help people implement lean manufacturing practices.

The OL Team also gave the plants seed money; one plant used the funding to produce a learning history. In addition, we facilitated communication among the participating plants and other organizations through tools such as dialogue and causal loop diagrams to help them better understand their current reality and align their efforts. The plant managers also knew they would need to "walk the talk" if they expected employees to get involved in implementing organizational learning (see "Walking the Talk"). To that end, five members of the manufacturing leadership attended the Organizational Learning Center's Executive Champion Workshop.

WALKING THE TALK

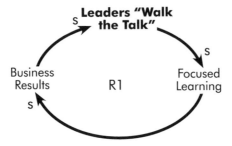

As leaders increasingly "walk the talk" in support of organizational learning concepts and tools, workers' learning rises. Enhanced learning then leads to an improvement in business results, which reinforces leaders' efforts to implement the principles of organizational learning.

Most plants worked with two external learning coaches. One learning coach from a U.S. plant partnered with local facilitators to help a European plant apply organizational learning methodologies. The need to train more learning coaches became critical as requests increased for support in implementing organizational learning. In response, 23 participants completed a 25-day coaching program that focused on a deeper understanding of the five disciplines. In addition, more than 20 people attended a workshop on the principles and key characteristics of learning histories and collective reflection skills.

As other parts of the company became aware of the manufacturing initiative, additional groups—including purchasing, product development, and information technology—requested support in implementing organizational learning. Because of the formal-informal infrastructure, which relied on local initiatives, the small OL Team was able to support a wide range of projects and more than 15 different groups.

Documenting Learnings and Results

Many teams documented their experiences with implementing organizational learning. The material included interviews, causal loop diagrams, and feedback forms capturing individual and collective reflection—all of which described the business impact of the learning applications. The documentation was key, because it gave us data to judge whether the implementation strategy was working, and it provided other groups with resources they could learn from (see "Key Learnings" on pp. 58–59).

According to the documentation, the organizational learning and reengineering effort yielded the following results:

- Dramatic quality improvements
- Enhanced understanding of current reality
- Improved management and union communications
- Stronger working relationships and a spirit of cooperation
- More open and honest communication
- Deeper understanding of important issues
- Less blaming behavior and greater understanding and collaborative problem-solving
- New ways to address complex issues

Because of these accomplishments, five additional plants and other reengineering teams have initiated learning projects. Also, some of the

---

KEY LEARNINGS

We believe that other companies can learn from our efforts. Therefore, we offer the following guidelines from our experience.

- **Ground the work in one or more important strategic initiatives within the organization.**

  Although it is useful for everyone in a company to know and live the five disciplines, this work ultimately must create value for customers, employees, and shareholders.

- **Don't do this work alone!**

  Form partnerships early on, so everyone participates in each step, from design to implementation. Partnering can greatly benefit both the change effort and the organization.

- **Promote the work through invitation.**

  Do not "roll out" organizational learning strategies and tools to everyone at once. Rather, introduce the concepts as part of a business initiative; people will accept the ideas more easily and will learn about them out of interest or necessity.

- **Be flexible concerning how people participate.**

  People learn in different ways, at different times, and at different rates. Therefore, offer a variety of ways for them to get involved. Some may benefit from formal training; others may prefer to acquire new skills while implementing organizational learning tools in their work.

- **Recognize both formal and informal leaders, and don't overlook sponsorship.**

  The most effective leadership comes from informal leaders within the organization. Because they may take great risks to do business in new ways, sponsors should be credible leaders who will stand up for what they believe.

(continued on next page)

---

participants in the coaching program have assumed active roles as learning facilitators within other divisions of Ford.

Questions for Further Inquiry

We believe that true wisdom lies in the question and not necessarily in the answer. Our efforts have raised many provocative and valuable questions, some of which we've listed below. In our view, these questions are relevant for other organizations and have the potential to inspire further inquiry and learning. You don't have to come up with answers to these queries for them to be of value; as one of our colleagues states, just let them flap in the wind for a while, like letting your laundry hang out to dry. You'll be surprised by the quality of thinking that may emerge!

KEY LEARNINGS, *continued*

- **Provide practice fields.**

  Give people the opportunity to practice the new tools and techniques in learning labs or in learning forums where individuals come together to discuss and rehearse different approaches. The environment must be safe and must allow for mistakes and failures as well as successes. Practice makes a real difference in both behavior and work outcomes.

- **Hold true to the quality and integrity of the effort.**

  Be alert for people who use the terminology but not the tools. Draw their attention to this lapse from a perspective not of punishment but of learning.

- **Be creative and use many different strategies.**

  Focus on generative learning across organizational boundaries. The OL Team used numerous strategies when implementing these concepts, which we continue to alter as we learn more. We keep the five disciplines as the foundation for our work, but we've also implemented learning histories, lessons learned, benchmarking, and learning forums.

- **Build capacity along the way.**

  Provide interested individuals with the knowledge and skills to use this material in their everyday work. Leverage external resources along the way, for experts can provide a fresh perspective and contribute to new theories and practices.

- **Remember that this work is relational.**

  Remember that you are trying to build good relations, which will in tur improve the quality of thinking. The goal is to learn and share, which people can do only if they respect one another.

- How do we build community in an organization that is profit-driven?
- How do we handle the issue of scale (moving from implementing these principles in 10 manufacturing plants to 180)?
- What is the role of leadership in this kind of effort, particularly if the philosophy is to let people make their own choices about their involvement?
- How do we sustain these efforts in a culture where there is high management turnover?
- What do people need to enhance personal and professional effectiveness?

This "flexible" strategy let us build on existing efforts and introduce new learning approaches and practices. As a result, we believe organizational learning practices will live on in Ford and will overcome the risk of being seen as one of many short-lived corporate initiatives.

Epilogue

The application of organizational learning theories, methods, and tools continues throughout Ford. Within Visteon, learning is viewed as an integral part of the way we achieve our business results and the way we behave with each other, our suppliers, and our customers. Learning coaches in each of the major functions play a role in creating practice fields for enhancing our learning skills; supporting focused learning efforts; and ensuring cross-boundary learning. A four-day Visteon learning course is offered in several locations, including Europe. Examples of some focused learning efforts include regular meetings with suppliers to build effective, long-term relationships; dialogue sessions in many of the leadership teams to create a shared understanding of business goals and to align actions to realize desired results; information exchanges between plants to learn how to accelerate lean manufacturing practices; and lessons-learned sessions to improve the process for quoting new business.

Many of Visteon's values and behaviors reflect a learning orientation, such as: take the enterprise view; have open, honest, and candid dialogue; trust and respect one another; take time to develop relationships with one another; and learn from your shared successes and failures.

We believe that the challenges we face today require a balance between a focus on managing to achieve the results and a focus on leading by the values. ⮌

Ann-Marie Krul was formerly the organizational learning manager for Ford's Process Leadership Office. She is presently the information technology and learning manager for the Climate Control Systems Division, Visteon Automotive Systems, Ford Motor Company.

Donald Mroz, PhD, is a partner in Waves of Change Partnership, an organizational development consulting firm. He is also an adjunct professor at the University of Michigan–Dearborn.

Team Learning at Kellogg Brown & Root: A New Process for Debriefing Projects

by Rebecca Johansson and Robert Spear

One of the hallmarks of the discipline of team learning, described by Peter Senge in his seminal book *The Fifth Discipline: The Art and Practice of the Learning Organization*, is that those who practice it continually learn together. For Kellogg Brown & Root, an international engineering and construction contractor, this means identifying the lessons from a challenging project and then applying them to the next project.

At Kellogg Brown & Root, we've developed a simple, fast project-debriefing process that captures the key lessons learned by all stakeholders involved in executing the project. This six-step process takes just one day to complete, and has been successfully applied to nearly 30 major projects that, together, have a total capital cost of more than $2.5 billion. The process is designed to help the contractor and its clients recognize the root causes of both the key success factors and major problems of large projects. Understanding these root causes is essential if we are to replicate successes on future projects and curb systemic problems on future projects—both of which are keys to client satisfaction and repeat business. Below we describe why we developed this innovative process, how we have implemented it on our projects, and what its benefits have been. We conclude with our thoughts about what constitutes a team learning process that can in turn contribute to the formation of a learning organization.

Setting the Stage

As a result of Dresser Industries' 1998 merger with Halliburton Company, The M.W. Kellogg Company merged with Brown & Root Engineering and Construction to form Kellogg Brown & Root. Headquartered in Houston, Kellogg Brown & Root is an international, technology-based engineering and construction company that provides a full spectrum of industry-leading services to the hydrocarbon, chemical, energy, forest products, and mining and minerals industries. We have approximately 23,000 employees.

We execute large, complex projects—and team learning is critical to our success. Typically, major projects involve the custom design of facilities to fit our clients' unique needs, procurement of the necessary equipment and materials, the erection of these materials at the job site, preparation of the erected facilities for start-up and operation, and sometimes operation and maintenance of the facility. These projects may require two to three years to complete and cost $25 million to $2 billion. Their success hinges on the careful coordination of more than 10,000 planned activities, which in turn are carried out by 20–500 engineers and specialists in the home office plus a construction workforce of 500–5,000 craftsmen.

Identifying the Need for a New Process

For many years, we had an effective process for identifying successes and problems on our projects within individual work groups within our project teams, and for disseminating this information. But as we began to make strategic improvements to our project-execution process in the early 1990s, we realized that capturing lessons learned within discipline silos left larger, more important lessons hidden. We knew we had to tailor our debrief process so as to view the project as a whole. So in May 1993, we began developing a new method that focused on capturing the *vital few* lessons from project successes and problems. This new process works effectively when clients are satisfied with our performance as well as when they are not.

Capturing Lessons Learned: The Process

We debrief projects either at the completion of the project or at the conclusion of a major execution phase (for example, at the end of the home office engineering and procurement effort). The process comprises six steps, and takes eight hours. Two facilitators guide senior representatives from the major stakeholders involved in executing the project (for instance, the client, Kellogg Brown & Root, key suppliers, and major sub-contractors) through the debrief.

Step 1: Clarifying Expectations. The goal of this first step is to cre-ate a safe "container" for skillful discussion and to make sure participants share the same mental model of the purpose of the debrief process. To begin building the container, participants develop their own ground rules governing expected behavior. The team encourages candor as well as respect for each participant. (That is, participants are coached to attack problems, not people.) The facilitators record the ground rules, along with expected behaviors, and then review them at the end of the day to gauge how well they have been followed.

The purpose of the debrief is to learn what went well on the project and what went wrong, and to understand why.

The facilitators' behavior, and the anonymity with which certain data is gathered, also helps create the safe container. To surface mental models, facilitators ask everyone, "What are you expecting to get out of today?" They especially watch for conflicting expectations; for example, some people might think the group is there to *identify* problems. Others may think it's there to *solve* them. In truth, the purpose of the debrief is to learn what went well on the project and what went wrong, and to understand why. Later, individual stakeholders will carry out their own debriefing process, within their organizations, to decide what kinds of concrete actions to take.

Step 2: Understanding Differences Between Initial Expectations and Actual Results. Over the years, we have discovered that project problems often stem from differences in mental models, or contrasting initial expectations of the client and the contractor. In Step 2, the debrief participants record what they expected from the project as well as what actually happened. Each person writes his or her impressions anonymous-ly on a Post-it Note™, and then places the completed notes on flipchart pages hung on the wall. Participants are not required to take ownership of their input until they feel ready.

Each flipchart page represents a major category of expectation. For example, client participants sort their expectations on flipcharts categorized by the main attributes of client satisfaction. Contractor participants categorize their notes according to the main attributes of how a client empowers a contractor to execute a project. Individual comments are grouped into like clusters. The client and contractor teams then develop a consensus opinion. Finally, the full project team reviews the material.

Often, this process reveals important but previously unrecognized differences in initial expectations among project team members. For example, one client expected that the contractor would prepare a front-end design package with minimal client involvement. Differences in mental models about what was to be included in the package led to rework and delays in the engineering work. Another example stemmed from incompatible assumptions within the client's operations and project teams about the project objectives and contract. In reality, significant misalignments existed that everyone involved failed to recognize initially. Understanding how these differences could arise in spite of the best efforts of both the client and contractor to prevent them is an important aspect of this team learning process.

Step 3: Recognizing Successes and Identifying Root Causes. The purpose of the third step is to identify the successful outcomes of the project, the key factors that contributed to these outcomes, and the key factors' root causes. Exploring these issues at this stage of the debrief sets a positive tone for the rest of the process. This step is also important because most project teams tend to focus more on their problems than of their successes. Even if a thousand things went well, highly motivated teams often rivet their attention on the few things that went wrong.

Typically, there are four to eight major successful outcomes associated with a project. Here are some examples from a recent endeavor: (1) project completed with an outstanding safety record, (2) project completed 11 weeks ahead of the contract schedule, (3) plant went on stream ahead of its competition and will achieve the client's business objectives, (4) repeat business is likely as a result of a very satisfied client.

We then ask participants to list what they see as the key success factors behind these outcomes on Post-it™ Notes. These notes are then placed on flipchart pages hung on the wall, and organized under the major project-execution phases. Next the project team consolidates similar responses into clusters. The team then determines the 12–15 most significant success factors for the project as a whole. Examples from one recent project (in no particular order) include: (1) very good teamwork occurred between the client and KBR, (2) client's operations requirements were met, and (3) early equipment and material delivery to the job site was provided by Procurement.

Next the facilitators help the project team identify cause-and-effect links between the most successful outcomes and key success factors. We then search for root causes of the success factors within the client's area of influence, and within the contractor's. Two root causes on a recent project were: (1) the client was willing to take a risk in using a different project-execution strategy and working relationship with the contractor, and (2)

We've discovered something interesting: Oftentimes, the project team is unaware of root causes of project problems.

---

the contractor's project-management team paid close attention to communication and people issues. We have found that the root causes of success tend to be well-known truisms. Nonetheless, it is very important to install mechanisms to ensure that these root causes are replicated on future projects.

Step 4: Recognizing What Went Wrong and Identifying Root Causes. Fortified by our assessment of what we did right, we can now move to identifying opportunities for improvement. This step is conducted using the same methodology as in Step 3. As in Step 3, participants record their individual perspectives and then consolidate them into a team consensus.

After conducting several debriefings, we've discovered something interesting: Oftentimes, the project team is unaware of root causes of project problems until they take part in this step. Furthermore, it turns out that root causes almost never derive from complex technical issues.

Instead, they usually stem from "soft" issues at a more macro level. For example, the root cause of problems in the client's arena on one recent project was their "project team staffing philosophy." In simplest terms, the client's contact people were not as available as the contractor needed them to be. In the contractor's arena, the root cause was "sequential, not parallel, execution of the engineering work," which caused rework and delays. Both root causes and their impacts went unrecognized until the debriefing process revealed them.

Step 5: Evaluating the Debrief Process. After spending almost an entire day talking, sharing, listening, and learning, it's time to take a few minutes to reflect and evaluate the debriefing process itself. In Step 5, participants compare the outcome of the debrief with their original expectations. They then share what they particularly liked or did not like about the session. Typically, they praise the skillful discussion, insightful learnings, variety of activities, the rapid pace of the day, and the opportunity for the client/contractor team to explore issues in a "win-win" atmosphere. On the other hand, some participants feel that certain issues are not made explicit enough, and want more time to plan concrete, corrective action. Just before we adjourn, participants also rate the effectiveness of the debriefing process on a 1-to-10 scale, with 10 meaning "outstanding." Client ratings typically exceed 8 on this scale. The facilitators use these responses to hone subsequent debriefing sessions.

Step 6: Creating the Report. After the debrief, the facilitators create a written report summarizing the lessons learned. This report documents the purpose of the debrief, and includes a short description of the project; the names of the participants; and both the individual and group findings regarding initial expectations, actual results, positive and negative project outcomes, key factors, and their root causes. Because the report contains everyone's input, all participants can feel confident that they have been heard, even if they did not share the majority opinion. This report is vital to our drive for continuous and accelerated improvement, because it transmits lessons learned from past projects and encourages reflection during the planning stages of subsequent projects.

Before distributing the report, both the client and contractor project managers review and comment on the draft. This review helps ensure that the final report accurately reflects the conclusions reached by the project team.

THE SIX-STEP PROJECT-DEBRIEFING PROCESS

1. Clarify debrief expectations.
2. Compare project expectations and actual results.
3. Identify successes and their root causes.
4. Identify problems and their root causes.
5. Evaluate the debrief process.
6. Document the debrief learnings.

The Benefits

How does this six-step process support team learning? As one important benefit, participants come to understand the project's successes and problems from a total project perspective, as well as grasp their individual contributions to them. The process also encourages people to look at their own behavior as a source of change instead of blaming other people or external circumstances for undesirable results. Ultimately, team members acquire a greater sense of trust in each other, and learn to leverage their strengths so as to preempt problems in future projects. Those who end up working on another project together can leverage that trust during the project itself and during the next debrief.

This team learning in turn benefits Kellogg Brown & Root and its clients. Following each debriefing, Kellogg Brown & Root's vice president of operations and his direct reports review a summary of the debriefing report. This gives them an opportunity to hear what our clients are saying (in their own words) about the work we have done for them, and to spot patterns in praise or complaints. This knowledge is then put to use in the company's strategic planning and improvement process.

Clients benefit, too. They have an opportunity to learn where and how they contribute to a project's successes or problems. Because this kind of in-depth, candid feedback is rare in the engineering-construction industry, it has earned high marks from our clients. Some of them even use the process to identify and spur corrective action in their own organizations.

All this means that our project debriefing process is also a key element in our client satisfaction strategy—a strategy designed to keep our clients coming back because we continually improve our performance and our ability to satisfy their needs.

Lessons from an Effective Learning Process

In our industry, as in any other, the clients and contractors who are able to learn together faster and better than the competition have a tremendous advantage. So it is important to understand what really makes an effective team learning process.

Our experience has shown us that a team learning process needs to be safe, fast, and effective. To be truly valuable, it must also generate constructive action. Here are the reasons why:

- *Safety.* This is essential to ensure that debate stays focused on issues, not on the people who raised them. (The use of Post-it Notes™ in our process achieves this nicely.)
- *Speed.* There is no room for a long, drawn-out, and expensive learning process in today's fast-moving business environment. Moreover, the people whose knowledge is needed for the debrief process are often not available except for short periods of time. (The one-day format in our process addresses this reality.)
- *Effectiveness.* Too many processes result only in a list of the "trivial many" successes and problems. As Peter Senge has explained, the most important learnings come from addressing entire systems. We must be able to isolate the "vital few" issues that truly drive success and problems. (The cause-effect analysis in our process helps us wade through the ocean of information related to a major project and distill it into the root causes of the most significant project outcomes—positive and negative alike.)
- *Action.* For true team learning to take place, an organization must use the learnings that it captures to respond differently to new challenges. Understanding without action is not learning. (Indeed, our process is directly tied to the company's strategic improvement initiatives.)

If all four of these elements—safety, speed, effectiveness, and action—are in place, a team will not only begin learning from its experiences, but the company will also be well on its way to becoming an effective learning organization. ✑

Rebecca Johansson is manager of communications for Kellogg Brown & Root, overseeing all internal and external programs designed to document and communicate the capabilities of the company and its people. Previously, she was a senior quality management specialist with The M.W. Kellogg Company, and focused on continuous improvement, communications, and learning. In this capacity, Rebecca was an internal consultant to management as it implemented strategic improvements in the areas of customer satisfaction, employee motivation, and work process improvement. Rebecca has a BS degree in English and speech from Houston Baptist University.

Robert Spear, PhD, is the director of quality for Halliburton Company. He leads the application of continuous improvement and quality management on a worldwide basis. Previously, he was the manager of quality for The M.W. Kellogg Company, where he was responsible for guiding the development of Kellogg's continuous improvement process. This industry-leading process integrates the synergistic principles found in systems thinking, theory of constraints, value management, and Total Quality Management. Robert has over 25 years of experience in streamlining project management, technical, and administrative operations. He has taught continuous improvement in the Executive Development Program and at the graduate level in the School of Business Administration at the University of Houston. He holds a doctorate in chemical engineering from Oklahoma State University.

Chapter Eight

Organizational Learning at Arthur Andersen: A Path for Improving Client Satisfaction

by James B. Rieley and Juan Garcia

Arthur Andersen Business Consulting is committed to developing consultants who are life-long learners and who can help clients achieve measurable performance improvement. As the new century approaches, we need to focus on how we will satisfy our mission by examining both what we do and how we do it. Organizational learning has proven to be a powerful tool in this effort.

Setting the Stage

Arthur Andersen Business Consulting (AABC) places a high priority on ensuring its clients' success and satisfaction. Like many companies, we occasionally struggle in trying to achieve this mission. For one thing, as our practice has grown (in terms of both revenues and headcount), we've experienced an influx of both new and experienced consultants who aren't able to "see" the vision of the practice. Our growth has also strained our monetary and physical resources. Finally, our need to support our growth has hampered our ability to strengthen our consulting capabilities.

Research has shown that, for an organization to improve its effectiveness, it must be able to learn, or "maintain or improve performance based on experience." This in turn requires the organization to support learning as a key value. To incorporate learning as a value, a consulting practice needs to take a hard look at certain structures related to the process of learning—specifically, policies and procedures, both explicit and implicit;

the stated goals of the practice; the mental models of practice members; and members' real and perceived ability to learn and perform.

Launching a Learning Initiative

In 1992–1993, AABC decided to explore organizational learning when it received some troubling survey results concerning its Operational Consulting practice (OC). The results showed that although OC did an excellent job of analyzing clients' problems and providing recommendations, it was less effective in helping clients implement change. Drawing inspiration from Peter Senge, who had emphasized that an organization's ability to change has a direct correlation to its ability to learn, AABC decided to launch a broad-based learning initiative throughout the company to improve client satisfaction.

The initiative began with a joint agreement between AABC and The Learning Circle to pilot an organizational learning (OL) course for all AABC consultants. The objective was to enable personnel throughout the company to acquire as much knowledge as possible and then share it with their colleagues at the local practices. In addition, AABC hoped to develop these learnings into a service line that it could package and deliver to clients.

The initial training provided by The Learning Circle consisted of a six-week, intensive practice field held over an eight-month period. Participants came from AABC practices in Houston, London, Tokyo, Kuala Lumpur, Amsterdam, Mexico City, Chicago, Buenos Aires, San Francisco, New York, Philadelphia, Boston, and Dallas. Attendees praised the training. However, they also worried that participants would have trouble applying their learnings to their own practices because of the complexity of the materials and the overall feeling that "you had to be there."

A Closer Look at the Learning Initiative: The Houston Practice

Despite these concerns, the members of AABC's Houston practice still wanted to move forward with the OL training because they firmly believed that it would mitigate the impact of Houston's growth—namely, the problem of decreasing alignment with the vision as the headcount at Houston grew. The figure "Investing in Learning at Arthur Andersen's Houston Practice" captures the Houston members' mental model of how investing in OL can help a company mitigate the impact of limits to its growth.

To see how this works, let's "walk" through the diagram. As the Houston practice has grown (R1), the number of new hires has also increased. But with more new hires, overall alignment with the organization's vision of ensuring client success has declined throughout the practice (B2). This lack of alignment threatened to blur the company's focus on client satisfaction, which would reduce client satisfaction, decrease the amount of new business coming in, and, ultimately, reverse Houston's growth. The practice believed that, to counteract this unpleasant scenario, it needed to invest in organizational learning—especially skills in the area of shared vision, one of the five OL disciplines. In this way, it could improve alignment with AABC's vision throughout the practice—thus mitigating the impact of the limits to Houston's growth (B3).

INVESTING IN LEARNING AT ARTHUR ANDERSEN'S HOUSTON PRACTICE

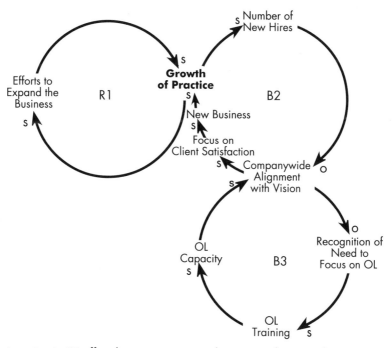

Investing in OL offered a way to mitigate the impact of a major limit to Houston's growth: the decline in companywide alignment with AABC's vision that came with an increase in new hires at the practice.

The two Houston practice members who had attended the firmwide training were eager to share their new knowledge with their colleagues. Inspired by the training, they envisioned an organization held together by a common purpose and vision and by a strong sense of individual accountability. Their goal was to clarify this vision so that all the Houston practice members could both see it and embrace it. For this to happen, they believed, new hires as well as longstanding practice members would need to continually improve their OL skills in practicewide training sessions.

In the mid-1990s, a training program was developed within Houston and distributed over two three-day sessions. The first session focused on the learning disciplines of personal mastery and mental models. The second session emphasized the disciplines of team learning and systems thinking. The goal was to strengthen the practice's three core competencies: *vision*, or the ability to clearly see a potential, desirable future for oneself and one's organization; *understanding*, or the ability to balance advocacy and inquiry in two-way communications; and *thinking in wholes*, or the ability to see systems holistically.

Both sessions generated some skepticism among participants at first. However, the uniqueness of the activities and the sessions' strong potential for personal growth also intrigued the participants. Despite some early misgivings, the program laid the groundwork for the dissemination of OL concepts, theories, and applications throughout the entire practice. Most important, the training helped the Houston practice members clarify a shared vision. In September 1995, the practice members met for three days to paint a mental picture of what they hoped the Houston practice would look like in the year 2000.

"Double-Loop Learning"

Owing to client needs, the Houston practice turned its attention to the growth of one of its practices in 1997, and its investments in OL diminished. This development had some potentially troubling ramifications, especially in light of the exponential growth that the practice had been experiencing. Accordingly, the Houston members decided to create a formal OL team charged with ensuring the continued delivery of OL training to new hires and the development of practice fields for more seasoned members who wanted to sharpen their OL skills.

The objective of this new team was to develop a methodology based on the model of double-loop learning. In double-loop learning, learners attend not only to *what* they're learning but also to *why* they're learning it (see "Double-Loop Learning"). In the case of the Houston practice, the "what" was OL skills. The "why" was that the practice would be able to strengthen its sense of shared vision, along with other skills, and thereby sustain and support its growth.

The Effort Bears Fruit

As the OL training continued at Houston, the practice members began to think about their business in new ways (see "Benefits of OL to the Houston Practice" on p. 76). Specifically, they started focusing on the organization's mission of ensuring client satisfaction. As a result, the sense

---

DOUBLE-LOOP LEARNING

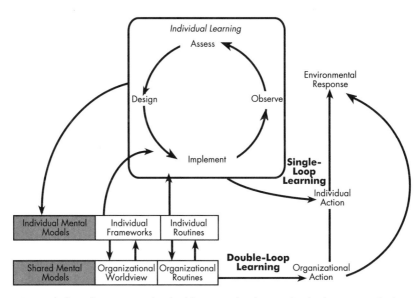

In single-loop learning, individual learning leads to individual actions, which generate environmental responses that generate more individual learning. In double-loop learning, the individual learning is leveraged collectively through shared understanding. It is this learning that leads to collective organizational actions that reinforce the learning process.

Source: Daniel H. Kim

BENEFITS OF OL TO THE HOUSTON PRACTICE

Before OL Training	After OL Training
Low ability to make recommendations "stick"	High level of implementation skills
Belief that working hard leads to success	Belief that learning leads to effectiveness
Belief that "this is the way we have always done it"	Belief in and support for innovative responses to client needs
Hierarchical structure driven by policies	Organizational structure based on client and consultant needs
A focus on hierarchy	An understanding of the dynamic relationships that influence practice effectiveness and capacity
Low levels of alignment and commitment	High levels of alignment and commitment
Narrow focus tied to processes	High understanding of systemic implications of actions
Mental model that OL is a "soft skill" and not as important as "hard," technical skills	Mental model that OL encompasses the foundational skill sets that are the basis for successful client work
Limited ability to "hear" clients and understand their needs	High capacity for understanding client mental models of what is important and why

of alignment with the practice's vision grew stronger. They also began seeing OL skills in a new light, a shift that helped them see the connections between OL and their ability to support their clients' success.

But how did the above benefits manifest themselves? These changes took the form of specific innovations in four key areas at Houston: Developing Knowledge-Sharing Structures, Developing People, Building Community, and Improving Consulting Skills. Below are some examples of these innovations.

Developing Knowledge-Sharing Structures: Knowledge-sharing structures are structures such as physical work-space arrangements and process flows that support the free exchange of knowledge between employees. At Houston, the practice members redesigned their work space to be open. In this redesign, dedicated offices were eliminated and replaced with a virtual office concept. Meeting, conference, and confidential "call" rooms were made available to all members through an on-line registration system. This new arrangement encouraged interaction among all members of the practice, and the resulting mingling of partners, managers, and consultants reduced the sense of hierarchy among the group.

Developing People: At Houston, people development means allowing employees to focus their work in areas where they are interested. For example, although the Houston practice members still have commitments to their usual clients (fees, proposals, deliverables, etc.), they also have opportunities to work on other projects, as long as they can keep meeting their original commitments. This flexibility has enhanced individual capacity at Houston as well as infused the practice with fresh ideas.

Building Community: AABC, the larger organization of which Houston is a part, consists of two former entities—the Business Systems Consulting group (BSC) and the Operational Consulting group (OC). When BSC and OC merged in mid-1995 to form AABC, the resulting blend of "cultures" offered AABC and its component practices some new advantages. BSC was very structured and technical. OC, on the other hand, was very flexible, a little less hierarchical, and more focused on the so-called "soft" skills of consulting. These characteristics of OC proved very beneficial to the AABC work environment, because they encouraged the contribution of each person rather than emphasizing titles. As a result, the new organization boasted a strong sense of community. This quality has given AABC and all its practices an important edge in sustaining their growth and success, for it attracts talented people who are looking for a unique place to enjoy a fruitful, fulfilling career.

Improving Consulting Skills: The Houston group adopted a wide range of OL tools in order to hone their consulting skills. For example, systems thinking, one of the five OL disciplines, fosters understanding of complex problems and provides a language with which to communicate about such problems with clients. Other tools from the discipline of team learning—such as dialogue, the ladder of inference, and the left-hand column—help participants steer conversations toward facts and away from assumptions and provide a framework for consultants to address tough issues with clients.

All these efforts to cultivate a learning environment have greatly improved Houston's effectiveness. The practice has been able to retain more and more top-quality consultants. Practice members appreciate the flexibility that comes with the Houston culture, and Houston's competitors are having a difficult time hiring people away. The OL training has also sparked new energy within the practice. Members now use a common vernacular for explaining the dynamics they encounter in engagements and feel a greater sense of self-confidence. Most important, they share a strong sense of alignment with the practice's stated purpose and are proving more effective than ever in their client work, as revealed by a client satisfaction survey.

The Organizational Learning Curriculum in Houston

Sustaining organizational learning training in the Houston practice requires an ongoing commitment—one that includes continually delivering high levels of client satisfaction. In a practice that has shown tremendous growth, both in revenues and in headcount, the commitment to OL training creates a healthy tension between the need to continually support new learning with the need to keep the number of billable hours high. Yet Houston understands that it is the ongoing training that fuels its capacity to satisfy its mission.

The current offering of OL training in the Houston practice reflects this commitment. It comprises 10 days of training, and has 120 employees—from partners and managers to consultants and support personnel—scheduled to participate. Keeping 120 employees from generating billable hours for 10 days is an impressive investment in the practice's growth and effectiveness.

The curriculum consists of several course modules that focus on the five learning disciplines as well as the design of practice fields and community building. The program's trainers and facilitators come from the Houston practice, signaling the importance of team learning and shared vision in a very visible way.

Spreading the Word

Can organizational learning help other AABC practices besides Houston? The outcomes seen in the Houston practice would suggest that the answer to this question is yes. However, the process is not easy. As we've seen, implementing the concepts, theories, and applications of OL requires an ongoing commitment from partners and takes practice members away from client work. Yet a practice that is not focused on ongoing learning—for all its members—will soon find itself struggling to meet its clients' needs. That's an outcome that few consulting companies can afford to risk. ⇗

James B. Rieley is a manager in the Arthur Andersen Business Consulting Knowledge Services Competency Center, and is located in Houston, TX.

Juan Garcia is a manager in the Business Operations Team of the Arthur Andersen Houston Business Consulting practice.

Chapter Nine

Redesigning Work Processes to Improve Customer Service

by Terry Cochran

Nationwide Insurance is the fifth largest property and casualty insurance company in the U.S. Several years ago, we began redesigning many of our business processes in an effort to reduce expenses while raising the quality of our service to customers. As with most insurance companies, we win customers based on the insurance rates we offer, and we keep customers based on the level of service we provide. Through market studies to determine what our customers expected from us, we learned that we had a way to go, in terms of both price and service, to satisfy them.

The redesign effort focused mainly on reshaping the work processes most associated with adding value to our customers. We found that the new processes let us handle the same volume of work with less operating expense and gave workers more ownership over their work. But getting the necessary support from employees and actually making the changes happen smoothly were major challenges.

Comparing Work Processes

New business and policy change and renewal transactions traditionally moved from one person to another. Each individual executed a specific task that was dependent on the work completed in the previous step. Workers were trained to perform only their particular functions. Each transaction typically involved a dozen or so main processes, with many hand-offs in between; for example, from incoming mail to distribution, to evaluation, to ordering reports, to underwriting, to updating the system, to typing, to mailing. The belief underlying this type of structure is that if individuals concentrate on performing specific tasks, they will become efficient at completing those tasks, and the processes will take care of themselves.

Based on our study, however, we determined that cross-training workers and organizing them into teams would increase productivity and enhance customer service. Each individual would learn to carry out most of the tasks required to complete a transaction. This new structure has four main processes, with very few hand-offs and considerably fewer job descriptions than in the previous structure. The teams are organized around the field sales organization generating the transactions, so workers have a sense of ownership of the transactions from start to finish.

This team-based process initially met with skepticism. Many people couldn't shake their conviction in the overriding efficiency of a functional structure made up of specialists. We needed "hard" evidence to convince employees at every level of the value of reorganizing our processes so dramatically. I turned to system dynamics modeling for help.

Using Simulation Models

In order to illustrate and compare the performance of a functional structure with that of a team-based structure, I built two *ithink*® simulation models (see "Specialists Versus Team Work Processes"). The Specialists model depicts groups of specialists processing transactions in a sequence of four steps, with each step dependent on the previous one. This model represents the way we traditionally processed transactions. The Team model depicts a team of multiskilled workers, with each worker performing all four steps, from the start of a transaction to the finish. Each model uses the same input and rate, and starts with the same number of pending transactions.

To compare the two simulations, we first ran them while keeping the time it takes to complete each step in the process constant. In this case, the end results of both models were exactly the same in terms of the cycle time to process transactions from start to finish and the total number of pending transactions. This parity occurred because there is no down time, or time when an employee is waiting for work, in either model under these circumstances.

SPECIALISTS VERSUS TEAM WORK PROCESSES

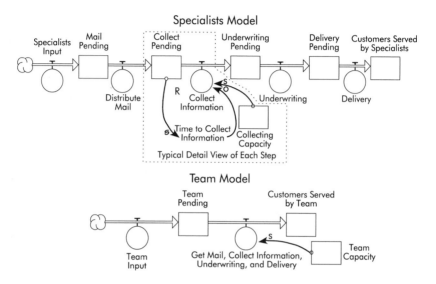

In the Specialists model, transactions pass from one specialist to another, with each worker performing a different function. If work is delayed at one step, it affects later steps. In the Team model, a multiskilled worker performs all four functions. This diagram shows a simplified version of the two models.

However, we also ran the models with variations in the time it takes to perform each step because, in the real world, some transactions take longer to process than others, and people are better at doing some tasks than others. With these variations, the Team model eventually excelled in terms of both the cycle time to process transactions and the total number of pending transactions.

So why does the Team model outperform the other? As work moves through the Specialists model, the specialists can work only on pending items in each of their queues plus any items passed to them from the previous step. When the time to complete a task varies, a specialist's current workload is sometimes less than the maximum that he or she can process, because transactions are delayed at a previous step. When such delays happen, the moment in time that the individual could have performed the "missing" transactions is lost forever, creating what is known as "idle capacity" (see "A Comparison of Idle Capacity" on p. 84).

A COMPARISON OF IDLE CAPACITY

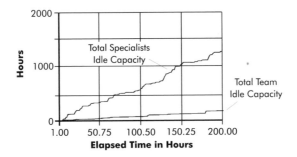

In the Specialists model, when transactions are delayed at a previous step, it creates "idle capacity." Idle capacity is far less in the Team model, because each worker can work on any pending item.

Because work continues to arrive, regardless of the fluctuations in the staff's ability to handle it, the number of pending items inevitably rises. The workers cannot catch up, because even though an individual at times works above average, the chain of specialists can perform no faster or more efficiently than its slowest member. As the number of pending transactions builds, the amount of time to process an order from start to finish also climbs. From the customers' perspective, the clock continues ticking, because in the Specialists model, lost time can never be recovered.

On the other hand, as work moves through the Team model, each multiskilled worker can perform work on any pending item. They too are able to complete more or less work at any given time. But because they are not dependent on the completion of previous steps by other workers, lower performance by one individual doesn't slow down the rest of the team. Someone who is working at an above-average rate at any given time will usually balance out someone working at a below-average rate. Cycle time and pending transactions can also rise in the Team model, but by less than in the Specialists model. When measured from the customers' perspective, there is less waiting time in the Team model because there are far fewer lost opportunities to complete a transaction than in the Specialists model (see "Additional Customers Served by Team Model").

ADDITIONAL CUSTOMERS SERVED BY TEAM MODEL

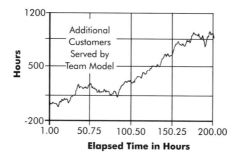

More customers are served in the Team model over time than in the Specialists model, because there are far fewer lost opportunities to complete a transaction.

This distinction is difficult for some people to grasp without viewing the models in action. If we were measuring success on the basis of the speed with which workers process each step, the measurements would be exactly the same for both models. But measurements taken from a customers' perspective yield quite different conclusions: The Team model is more efficient in processing orders from start to finish. By defining the process as both starting and ending with the customer, what matters is the efficiency of each transaction and not the individual results of each step in the process.

These models also reveal that it takes time for the differences between the two structures to become obvious. Over the short term, there is no significant difference between the two models in the time it takes to process an item or in the number of pending transactions. In fact, because of the fluctuations built into the simulation, the Specialists model occasionally outperforms the Team model. But after running several iterations, the Team model is clearly more productive from the customers' perspective.

Identifying Key Implementation Issues

In addition to convincing people of the benefits of the new work processes, the models also led us to identify other considerations. For example, we asked ourselves, Is it reasonable to expect multiskilled workers to become as efficient as specialists? What about the added cost of training and paying someone who is capable of handling more than one skill effectively? How will this change affect turnover and learning curves? Isn't it a waste of resources to ask a skilled technician to perform clerical functions?

The answer to all these questions is that it depends on the lead time for implementation, the cost of resources, management's commitment, the

---

By bringing our assumptions out on the table through the use of models, we addressed what might happen.

---

complexity of the tasks, and more. The important thing is to identify these issues and make sure the implementation plan takes them into account. By bringing our assumptions out on the table through the use of models, we addressed what might happen. We freed ourselves from deeply held beliefs that may no longer be appropriate for us, discussed the undiscussables, managed our assumptions within the context of a new process, and measured our success from the customers' perspective.

The results of the simulations may seem like common sense. But if you are a manager or a worker in a center undergoing process redesign, you may not be prepared to accept another way of working without proof of its value. The models help respond to "I'll believe it when I see it," because you can see "it" in the behavior of the simulation.

Implementing the Process Redesign

During the implementation phase of the process redesign, we used the models to educate people as to why we were making changes in work processes. For people already working in teams, the models served to reinforce their current practices. For others, the models powerfully demonstrated the benefits of the process redesign to workers, customers, and the company as a whole. Most people became convinced that the team-based system of multiskilled workers was the best way to enhance efficiency and customer service.

Implementing the new process has taken longer than we anticipated, principally because of the length of the learning curves as workers are cross-trained and assume additional responsibilities. For example, people who previously performed strictly clerical functions are now being asked to handle telephone calls from customers; others who have provided customer service are now also performing some underwriting tasks.

As part of the implementation process, we created a final, more complex model of the actual processes that includes "what-if" simulation modeling capability. If used properly, these models could help managers prepare budgets and determine staffing needs. So far, we have found that people are more comfortable working with internal consultants on the models.

We continue to use models primarily to demonstrate concepts, define goals, and obtain buy-in. We have found that when dynamic simulation models are used in conjunction with traditional approaches, such as static diagrams and descriptive documents, they add the realism needed to create a shared understanding at the operational level. Sometimes that realism is exactly what it takes to generate the confidence to move boldly forward. ⮌

Terry Cochran is an internal consultant with the Nationwide Insurance Property Casualty Company. He holds an undergraduate degree in math education from the University of South Dakota and an MBA from the University of Dayton. He also has a Chartered Life Underwriter Insurance designation from the American College.

Chapter Ten

Systems Thinking: A Tool for Organizational Diagnosis in Healthcare

by Diane L. Kelly

Advances in diagnostic technologies have given healthcare clinicians the ability to see deeper into the human body. We can now analyze cells almost at the molecular level, and we can see the body in two-dimensional pictures. Combining "high-technology" diagnostic tools, such as magnetic resonance imaging, with "low-technology" diagnostic tools of asking, looking, listening, and feeling, allows healthcare clinicians to understand a human system in ways unparalleled in the history of medicine. Similarly, new technologies of organizational diagnosis are providing healthcare leaders with tools that, when combined with traditional management techniques, can help us understand the complexities of organizations operating in today's healthcare environment.

At Intermountain Health Care, we have found systems thinking to be a valuable tool. This methodology has given us a new perspective with which to understand the multifaceted nature of our organization. It has also helped us evaluate operating strategies to determine whether they support quality patient care and long-term cost effectiveness. This chapter presents an overview of what initially motivated us to take a systems approach, describes our story using systems archetypes, and explores the value in using systems thinking as an alternative to traditional linear analysis.

Setting the Stage

Intermountain Health Care (IHC) is an integrated-care delivery system that includes 23 hospitals, a physician division, and a health-plans division. We provide healthcare services to communities throughout Utah, Wyoming, and Idaho. For the past 10 years, the state of Utah has outpaced the national average in job creation. The state has also shown strong population growth over the past six years. Along with this growth, Utah has one of the lowest unemployment rates in the country.

Our organization has also experienced expansion in the number of patients seen in our facilities and the number of enrollees in our health plans. After years of declining hospital occupancy, we have recently struggled to keep up with the need for hospital beds and staff. And because desirable jobs are so plentiful in our area, we have found employees difficult to recruit and have experienced high turnover rates across departments.

We also are part of an industry that is shifting toward downsizing and "downskilling" healthcare employees. Some healthcare organizations have sought to control the costs of health services by using entry-level employees for some tasks instead of highly trained—and more expensive—professionals. IHC has been affected by all of these trends.

Shifting to a Systems Approach

My colleagues and I worked on two projects intended to make a hospital in our organization more efficient—one project involved outpatient surgery; the other, laboratory services. While working on the projects, we came to the conclusion that, in some cases, the hospital could cut costs and better meet patients' expectations by using higher educated and higher paid staff instead of entry-level employees. In the outpatient surgery unit, for example, we found that we could reduce cost per patient by 14 percent by retaining an all-professional staff to carry out a reengineered patient-flow process.

This counterintuitive finding led us to focus on the difficulty of recruiting professional staff, particularly in areas requiring specialized clinical education and experience. For example, even with national recruitment efforts, it can take up to a year to hire qualified ultrasound technologists. This relatively recent phenomenon—combined with the high turnover of entry-level employees over the past several years—raised questions about the nature of our labor resources; our ability to recruit, hire, and retain qualified staff; and the implications of turnover for patient satisfaction, clinical outcomes, and costs.

Because of the complexities involved in addressing these trends, we decided to use a new set of resources to examine the issues. Systems

---

Systems thinking provided us with the language and tools to put down on paper what many of us were observing and feeling intuitively.

---

thinking provided us with the language and tools to put down on paper what many of us were observing and feeling intuitively. We began using a systems perspective and the systems archetypes to examine the labor issues of one hospital in the organization.

Developing the Story

Through interviews of employees in a variety of roles and departments, a picture of our organization's structure began to emerge. The process was iterative: Based on the conversations with different staff members, I created diagrams of the system. I then shared the figures with those same individuals, who made additional contributions to the story. As people became more and more enthusiastic about the insights captured by the systems diagrams, they asked me to share the drawings with their managers.

This discovery process opened doors through which people communicated a viewpoint to their supervisors that not only reflected the system as a whole but also included their own perspectives. The systems story became the language, individual conversation became the vehicle, and I became a messenger who helped open communication among several levels in the organization.

Using Systems Archetypes. We created a final diagram depicting our organization's structure (see "Unintended Consequences and

UNINTENDED CONSEQUENCES AND HIDDEN COSTS

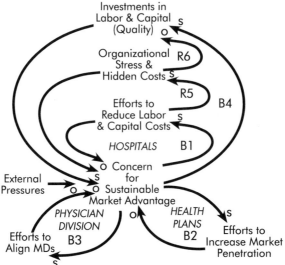

The three divisions' strategies are shown in loops B1, B2, and B3. The short-term fix for controlling rising costs is to decrease labor and capital costs (B1). But the fundamental solution is to increase investment in labor and capital to meet the demands resulting from enrollment increases and population growth (B4).

Hidden Costs"). The overall strategies of the three divisions in the organization—hospitals, physicians, and health plans—are depicted in three balancing loops (B1, B2, and B3). Yet the top of the diagram let us explore an even deeper issue: the unintended consequences of a cost-cutting strategy that seeks to reduce labor costs by decreasing the ratio of professional/licensed staff to total department staff (R5). These unplanned consequences are shown as the variable "Organizational Stress and Hidden Costs." Organizational stress is defined as straining or stretching resources beyond a proper limit. The indicators used to measure the level of organizational stress include turnover rate, rookie factor, workload, and employee satisfaction. Hidden costs comprise the money and time needed to train new employees to full productivity.

The interrelationships of these variables resemble the systems archetypes "Fixes That Fail" (B1, R5) and "Shifting the Burden" (B1, B4, and

R6). The short-term fix for controlling rising costs is to *decrease* invest-ment in labor and capital. But the fundamental solution is to *increase* investment in labor and capital in order to meet the additional demands on the hospital resulting from enrollment increases and population growth. In the diagram, we have also included the variable "External Pressures," which includes market competition, payer/employer pressure, and government policy.

Understanding the Systemic Structure. This diagram helped us understand how we might be undermining our own ability to hire pro-fessional staff. It also opened up other areas of inquiry. We have learned that, because some local schools decide their enrollments based on the current number of job openings in a particular field, hospital staffing decisions made today can affect the number of qualified job applicants available in four to five years. For example, from 1994 to 1996, local hos-pitals aggressively reduced positions for registered nurses. Applications for enrollment at a local nursing school dropped by 41 percent during the same time period.

We have also started to look at age distribution data for different positions in the organization. We found that 83 percent of medical tech-nologists at one hospital are older than 40; 11 (14 percent) are over 55 and are eligible for retirement. We then did some research and discovered that, in 1997, only 14 medical technologists graduated from the local school, which feeds employees to all of the area hospitals and nonhospi-tal laboratories. By looking at our hospital and the surrounding commu-nity from a systemic perspective, we have begun to get a sense of the future impact of our current decisions on the wider community. As a result of these insights, our organization has started to work with local schools to cultivate future medical technologists.

The Value of a Systems Approach

We have found that systems thinking provides more than a set of tools. It also offers a broader perspective on issues, as exemplified by our changing use of data. Before we learned about the systems archetypes, we examined the issue of labor resources using only traditional financial data and statis-tics. The relationships depicted in our causal loop diagrams encouraged us to explore variables that we would not have previously considered, such as indicators of organizational stress. We have also learned the importance of analyzing data from a variety of viewpoints—both aggregated to represent the system as a whole and "drilled down" to reflect groups within the system.

A systems approach has also encouraged us to broaden our original investigation into labor trends. We have since come up with additional queries about labor resources, such as:

- What is the threshold of organizational stress that, when met, begins to compromise patient satisfaction and clinical outcomes, and drives labor out of our work force?

- By intentionally decreasing professionals as a percentage of the total work force over the last few years, have we sent an unintended message that the demand for nurses and other professionals is declining? How long will it take to reverse that perception in the labor pool?

- What are the implications resulting from the compounding effect of new hires—the "rookie factor"—across departments and disciplines?

In addition to these new questions, a systems perspective has helped us identify the interrelationships of other important variables in our organization. Although our inquiry initially focused on one hospital, more general implications for managing an integrated-care delivery system began to emerge. For example:

- IHC has three divisions and multiple sites, each with different rules, histories, participants, and cultures. Systems thinking can help us understand how the parts of a complex system can effectively work together to accomplish the goals of the entire system—without sacrificing the goals of the individual parts. It is important to understand that "integrated" does not mean "same." Some divisions or sites may have different needs based on geographic location, patient populations, services offered, and so on. Translating high-level strategy into operational reality requires an understanding of the commonalities as well as individuality of each entity within the system and the manner in which the entities are connected.

- The organization must align its division goals and strategies, with careful attention to unintended consequences, both within and between divisions. For example, well-intended human-resource policies regarding pay or benefits may actually siphon staff from one part of the organization to another by making it just as financially rewarding to work in a low-stress area as in a high-stress area of care delivery.

- The organization should take care when allocating resources so as to support growth in a particular area. It must balance needs so that short-term strategies do not create an irreparable "Shifting the Burden" scenario for individual sites in the organization.

Summing Up

Although our organization has not yet determined any decisive strategies based on our systems analysis, I am confident we have made better decisions because of the early opportunities for dialogue and new perspectives provided by systems thinking. For example, we have begun to take into account the hidden costs associated with turnover and will focus on lessening turnover as part of an effort to reduce costs and maintain appropriate levels of staffing.

With patients, treating an underlying disease can yield a much more positive outcome than simply treating the symptoms. Similarly, with organizations, treating fundamental problems and addressing underlying structures can provide high leverage for addressing systemic problems. Diagnosis is key in both arenas. We have found that systems thinking provides the tools and language necessary to understand and diagnose the challenges our organization faces in today's complex healthcare environment.

Epilogue

Systems thinking can often serve as a tool for diagnosis, as well as for the stimulation of dialogue between diverse groups of people inside and outside an organization. Specifically, I have discovered that the archetypes tell stories so effectively that, in the case of Intermountain's learning journey, listeners have consistently asked me to tell the story again and again—and to share it with others. This iterative process has continued at Intermountain through one-on-one conversations, small-group discussions, and group presentations. Indeed, the Intermountain story has been told to and discussed among well over 150 people at all levels within the organization.

The story and its accompanying data, presented in combination with published research on the topics of failure and error, have led the administrative group at Intermountain to reevaluate policies on allocating human resources. A monthly report was also developed for managers, so that they could monitor the level of organizational stress

---

I discovered that because systems thinking tools demand a broad view of the issues in question, this larger view in turn had relevance for a wider, community audience.

---

at their own departmental level. Folks within the organization told folks outside about the story. I was invited to tell it to students in healthcare administration and nursing administration programs at two different local universities, at the annual meeting of the state organization of nurse executives, and at the state health policy commission. I discovered that because systems thinking tools demand a broad view of the issues in question, this larger view in turn had relevance for a wider, community audience. What started as dialogue between managers and administrators within one organization expanded to dialogue among educators, managers, and policy makers throughout the state of Utah.

This expanded dialogue has also provided the opportunity to take the story deeper. As the audience for the story has grown, I have studied the responses of the listeners, looking for common themes and patterns. Throughout this process, I identified a deeper, underlying structure that can help healthcare organizations maintain quality clinical and performance outcomes (see "Going Deeper: The New Story"). In the ever-growing complexity of the healthcare industry, the impact of traditional hierarchies and limited information flow can have devastating effects. However, the environment is also ripe for collaboration, participation, and information sharing—up, down, and across all levels of the organization. It is through such sharing that virtuous cycles can arise to enhance quality outcomes. ⟜

GOING DEEPER: THE NEW STORY

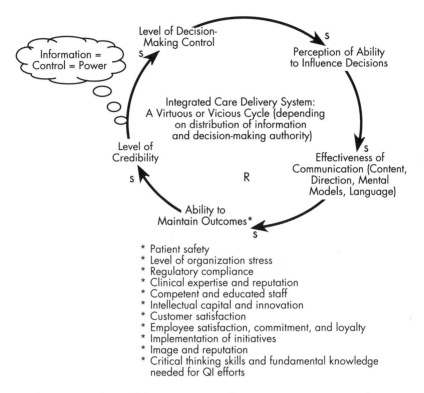

Level of Decision-Making Control

Information = Control = Power

s

Perception of Ability to Influence Decisions

s

Integrated Care Delivery System: A Virtuous or Vicious Cycle (depending on distribution of information and decision-making authority)

Level of Credibility

s

R

Effectiveness of Communication (Content, Direction, Mental Models, Language)

s

Ability to Maintain Outcomes*

s

* Patient safety
* Level of organization stress
* Regulatory compliance
* Clinical expertise and reputation
* Competent and educated staff
* Intellectual capital and innovation
* Customer satisfaction
* Employee satisfaction, commitment, and loyalty
* Implementation of initiatives
* Image and reputation
* Critical thinking skills and fundamental knowledge needed for QI efforts

The integrated care delivery system can be a virtuous or vicious cycle.

Diane L. Kelly was project leader for redesign efforts in the Urban Central Region of IHC. She combines her clinical and business backgrounds to integrate innovative management tools within the healthcare context.

The author would like to thank Michael Goodman of Innovation Associates for sharing his thinking and for teaching the tools used to pursue this inquiry. She would also like to acknowledge Matt Scott, administrative intern, whose collaboration and insights fostered the documentation of the initial story.

Chapter Eleven

Simulating a Classroom for Increased Student Achievement

by Jorge O. Nelson

Businesses today commonly employ computer simulations in learning laboratories to achieve systemic improvements and train employees in systems thinking. Similarly, using computer simulation tools to model an educational system represents one of the most exciting strategies for improving quality in schools today. At the American School of Durango, Mexico, we have implemented a computer simulation in staff development exercises to enhance the body of knowledge our teachers bring into the classroom. In an unexpected—and welcome—consequence, the simulation has also provided a new form of communication among colleagues and between teachers and the administration. We have found that the use of a computer model to enhance communication within a school or a business can be a powerful way to support the goals of organizational learning.

Teacher Behavior and Student Achievement

The relationship between teacher behavior and student achievement represents the foundation of any educational system. By their actions in the classroom, educators can have a profound influence on students' performance. But reading the wealth of research findings on this subject can be a tedious and confusing ordeal. The chapter dedicated to teacher behavior and student achievement in the Handbook of Research on

Teaching, which formed the basis of the simulation that we use, comprises 47 pages of single-spaced text and 205 citations. The body of research in itself is an invaluable tool for educators, but they find the conclusions easier to absorb in a 15- to 30-minute simulated session.

This simulation provides educators with a way to experiment with processes that take place in the classroom without causing stress to students, teachers, or any other part of the real-world system.

The computer model simulates how different teacher behaviors, such as giving praise or allowing students to call out answers, affect student achievement. This simulation provides educators with a way to experiment with processes that take place in the classroom without causing stress to students, teachers, or any other part of the real-world system. Teachers, administrators, and researchers can see the "big picture" as they manipulate the research-based findings in the "microworld" of a simulated classroom.

Construction of the Model

At the American School, we support a teaching methodology known as the Instructional Theory into Practice (ITIP) direct instruction model. Using ITIP, the teacher delivers new knowledge to students, checks for understanding by soliciting responses to questions, and lets students demonstrate mastery of the new learning through independent practice exercises. I used direct instruction as a theoretical basis for the simulation and based the correlations in the computer model on an accepted synthesis of research-based findings about the effects of teacher-student interaction. For instance, research shows that when teachers wait about three seconds after asking a question before allowing responses, students' academic achievement is enhanced over the long run.

I constructed the simulation in the *ithink*® system dynamics modeling language on an Apple Macintosh laptop computer. I chose *ithink*®

because of the wealth of available documentation and support material, and the ease of programming in the Macintosh computer operating system. After completing the model, I conducted two validation studies to confirm the accuracy of the output.

The simulation encompasses twelve variables in four different categories of teacher behavior: giving information, questioning students, reacting to student responses, and handling seatwork and homework. It also incorporates variables that address characteristics of students and teachers. Variables involving instructors include years of experience, organizational skills, and expectation bias. Variables focused on students include socioeconomic status and grade level. Research has shown that teacher behavior can have different effects on student achievement in lower and upper grades as well as in higher and lower socioeconomic status levels. For instance, praise elicits a more positive response from younger children than from their older counterparts. The complex interrelationships among all these variables form the basis for the simulation (see "Using the Simulator" on p. 102).

Implementation of the Simulation

We use the computer simulations in several different ways at the American School:

Orientation. We use this model during orientation for new teachers to create a risk-free environment that lets them experiment with strategies for increasing student achievement without actually entering a classroom. Novice teachers attempt to increase their "scores" by playing the simulation—or isolated parts of it—in sessions with or without the support of a master teacher or principal. The user can stop the sessions at any time, allowing the facilitator to intervene when necessary.

The simulation provides a nonthreatening environment where teachers and administrators can focus on new techniques and begin a dialogue about ways to improve the educational process. Although the whole process lasts only 15 to 30 minutes, the instructor learns new strategies, the administrator helps train a new staff member, and both develop a shared language regarding systemic change.

Staff Development. For veteran teachers, we use the simulation to introduce or reinforce the research regarding increasing student achievement. These experts use the program to try different approaches for opti-

USING THE SIMULATOR

Teachers begin the session by watching an example of a worst-case educational scenario played out over the course of a simulated academic year (see "The Dashboard"). This sample session depicts the results of a novice teacher who is implementing ineffective instructional strategies. Graphs over a period of 180 school days show that this teacher's students average only 13 percent of possible academic achievement. The teacher also suffers from burnout caused by overwork and stress.

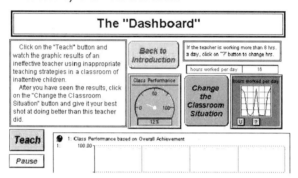

After watching the results of ineffective classroom behaviors, users are prompted to implement changes in strategies to improve student achievement. They change the values of the variables in the model, such as the amount of praise given by the instructor, and then view the graphs that reflect student performance. When teachers are not sure of which way to adjust strategies to improve achievement for a given classroom situation, they can access expert findings about effective teaching. The session usually takes about 15 to 30 minutes from start to finish.

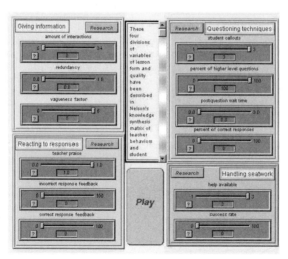

mizing student performance. For example, a veteran teacher who previously allowed students to call out answers to questions learned the benefit of having students raise their hands and wait to be called on. She now realizes that many students need time to formulate their responses. Teachers can suspend a simulation session at any time during the "school year," reflect on their choices, and modify the teaching behaviors they've selected if the immediate results do not indicate sufficient increases in achievement. The simulation session then begins again where it left off.

Supervisor Assessment. We use the simulation in the area of supervisor and administrator assessment to ascertain whether principals have a sufficient knowledge of the relevant research to observe and identify teaching behaviors effectively when evaluating instructors. For example, our principals run the simulation and observe specific simulated teacher behaviors as well as the resulting level of student achievement. After the session, the principals give recommendations for how the "virtual" teacher could improve his or her performance; for example, by giving students time to formulate their answers to questions. The principals then view their recommendations in action to see if they accurately evaluated the teacher's behavior. We also use this model as a tool for training administrators about state-of-the-art teaching methodologies.

Most staff members have found the simulation useful. A veteran sixth-grade teacher remarked, "I feel that it was a quick and fun program that helped me examine the learning process in my classroom. It helped me pinpoint a couple of things I can do differently to improve the achievement level. Specifically, I'm thinking about how I check for understanding." Another instructor commented, "It . . . helped me [think about] the percentage of students that understand a concept, watching each day for their responses." In general, users have found value in the computer model and feel that student-teacher interactions can be usefully simulated.

Learning Laboratories in Education

Learning laboratories are designed to create an environment in which educators can step back from day-to-day demands to reflect on their decision-making process; develop a common vocabulary; learn new tools for thinking systemically; discuss educational objectives and strategies in an open forum; test educational assumptions; experiment with new policies and strategies; and have fun.

The second purpose listed above—to develop a common vocabulary among participants—is a key benefit to using a computer model. Simulations help students, teachers, administrators, and researchers formulate and apply shared terminology for certain classroom behaviors. The model has also improved communication among instructors and between staff and administration, bringing to light differing perspectives. In addition, instructors have a renewed interest in the educational process; much of the talk in the teachers' room now centers on the value of different classroom strategies. An additional benefit is that teachers and administrators have gained a basic understanding of the principles of system dynamics.

Schools as Learning Organizations

Simulations such as the one presented here allow schools to draw closer to becoming what Peter Senge calls learning organizations. Traditional organizations emphasize independence of an enterprise's individual parts, including individuals, departments, and management. Learning organizations, on the other hand, recognize and celebrate interdependencies among the system's various components.

To achieve meaningful educational reform, schools must break out of static, linear, cause-and-effect modes of thinking and begin to think in systemic, circular, holistic terms. By cultivating the disciplines of organizational learning—especially systems thinking—educational institutions can focus more clearly on the interdependent "webs" of relationships that make up their system. The link between teacher behaviors and student achievement is just one of many of these relationships.

Our use of the simulator has shown that "soft" variables, such as academic achievement and specific teaching strategies, can easily be modeled. The advantages we've found in using the simulation—such as an increase in the skill level of our teaching staff and improved communication between instructors and administrators—are transferable to the business world. Such models can prove invaluable for training new and existing employees and for improving worker productivity in continuous improvement efforts.

Epilogue

Since the publication of "Simulating a Classroom for Increased Student Achievement" in *The Systems Thinker* Newsletter in April 1998, I've experienced a number of additional outcomes using two system dynamics simulations—SimClassroom and SimBudget—in educational settings. I am currently superintendent of Anzoategui International School in Anaco, Venezuela. AIS is a private, overseas, accredited (U.S.-curriculum based) K–12 school on the border of the Amazon jungle. I recruit teachers from the States to work and live in Venezuela for a minimum two-year contract.

This unique working environment lends itself to a different approach in recruiting staff members. Annual international school recruitment fairs are a two- to three-day marathon event, whereby each of the heads of schools meets up to 60 candidates in 30-minute interviews and makes rapid decisions that directly affect the schools for the next two years. Recruiting heads become overwhelmed by the sheer numbers of candidates and can make hasty decisions, many times regretting such haste later.

I have begun using the SimClassroom simulator, previously described as a teacher-training tool, in recruitment interviews as well. Teacher candidates sit with me in short, 10-minute sessions and "fly the classroom." I observe not only the output (increase/decrease in student achievement "scores") of the simulator but also the demeanor of the teacher during the simulation.

The process has proven to be an icebreaker, and candidates have generally been more accessible and communicative when focusing more on running the simulation than on impressing the superintendent per se. I get a sense of the amount of learned research candidates bring to the table, as well as candidates' style and personality. I also observe them "flowing" through the interview rather than getting stuck in trying to make a great first impression. More often than not, we hire more mission-appropriate teachers for our particular school environment and educational philosophy.

Another system dynamics simulation that has helped me improve schools is SimBudget. This is a budget simulator that takes into consideration a number of seemingly disparate financial variables. It then brings these parts into a synergistically aligned model of school finance in international settings.

Many international schools function under unique financial conditions, including dual currency issues (U.S. dollars and local currency), wild inflationary and interest swings, devaluation, and chaotic national elections; not to mention growing global influences and environmental issues. SimBudget takes a yearly budget prediction and plugs in all of the above variables and more. It then outputs scenarios so that accountants, board members, and superintendents can grasp how these diverse conditions affect the bottom line. The simulator lets "nonbusiness-type" decision-makers easily predict cash flow. SimBudget is not designed to give "the answer," but to bring a cadre of interested parties together to discuss/design/build/play with numbers in a game-like manner. In this way, they can break down barriers and build teams at the same time. ∽

Jorge O. Nelson was the director general of the American School of Durango, Mexico, and is now the superintendent of Anzoategui International School in Anaco, Venezuela. He holds an undergraduate degree in education from Evergreen State College, an MA in curriculum and teaching from Michigan State University, and a doctorate in educational leadership from the University of Memphis. He welcomes your comments and suggestions for improving schools overseas and elsewhere.

SimClassroom and SimBudget are two quality tools that have been found to help create quality schools. You can learn more about these tools by visiting www.hbcybernetics.com (http://www.hbcybernetics.com/).

Chapter Twelve

A Systems View of Communicating Change: The Navy Acquisition Reform Team

by Alex Bennet

How does an organization responsible for providing all the ships, airplanes, and weapon systems for the Department of the Navy respond to major budget and manpower cuts? To sustain future capability, the Navy's acquisition system had to shift its way of thinking and learn new ways of doing business. Systems thinking and organizational learning were key factors in this change process. The approach used for this transition offers lessons to all complex organizations in both the public and private sectors (see "Strategy for Communicating Change" on p. 108).

The U.S. Department of the Navy (DoN) acquires weapon systems through a complex acquisition system that consists of a workforce of more than 50,000 people, numerous departments, and many private firms. Acquisition activities include research and development of new systems, production, testing and evaluation, and in-service support. The acquisition system has evolved over a 50-year period, much of it during the Cold War. Driven by this environment, the Navy developed a complex set of rules and policies that ensured high quality—and high cost— state-of-the-art weapons. Of late, greatly reduced funding and staffing cuts have prompted the department to seek ways to do things more efficiently and effectively.

STRATEGY FOR COMMUNICATING CHANGE

To ensure success in implementing Acquisition Reform (AR), the Acquisition Reform Office designed a strategy to:
- Communicate top-level Navy support for rapid implementation of AR
- Focus and facilitate reform efforts through a change agent
- Link AR to ongoing changes across the system
- Build a continuous dialogue with industry to identify mutually beneficial opportunities and practices
- Facilitate rapid implementation of AR objectives by removing barriers and impediments to change
- Identify and deploy key process and product innovations
- Widely communicate expectations, successes, and lessons learned
- Institutionalize change management within the Navy acquisition culture to ensure flexibility and long-term improvement.

Initiating Reform Efforts

In January 1994, the DoN jumped full-strength into reforming its acquisition system by chartering the Acquisition Reform Office. The objective of Acquisition Reform (AR) is to achieve the Department of Defense's goal of military superiority at lower cost with increased customer satisfaction. In this case, the customers are sailors, marines, and, ultimately, U.S. citizens. Key elements of the reform effort include utilizing commercial processes and products, encouraging innovation, fostering managed risk, promoting empowerment of the acquisition workforce, and establishing cross-functional teams using world-class industry practices. To ensure cultural change, communication and education and training initiatives were instituted throughout the system. The intent was to reach every individual in the acquisition workforce.

Building on Success

Recognizing that success begets success, the Acquisition Reform team sought to create—and then promote—early successes. "The Communication Success Loop" shows the importance of carefully selecting initiatives that have a high probability of success; an initial success can trigger a "virtuous" reinforcing loop, while a failure can cause the loop to run in a "vicious" direction. Thus, as the number of changes

THE COMMUNICATION SUCCESS LOOP

As the number of changes grows, the amount of new information rises, leading to an increase in the amount of information sent and received. Increasing the flow of information and improving the quality of communication has a positive impact on the level of effective communication, which in turn drives "good feelings" and support for change (R1).

grows, the amount of new information rises, leading to an increase in the amount of information sent and received. Increasing the flow of information and improving the quality of communication has a positive impact on the level of effective communication, which in turn drives "good feelings" and support for change (R1).

The Acquisition Reform team implemented the following strategy to create and leverage positive changes:

Highlight Top-Level Commitment. As an important first step, the AR team communicated the commitment of senior leaders to the implementation of AR. To do so, a senior oversight council was set up to encourage dialogue on new ideas and to facilitate the regular exchange of AR information throughout the Department of the Navy. The entire acquisition workforce participated in a one-day stand-down to focus on how to improve operations. Historically, military stand-downs (where every member of the organization stops normal operations) have been called when a major problem had to be fixed. This stand-down focused

on strategic planning to reduce costs. To demonstrate their commitment to AR, senior leaders personally participated in the stand-down,
addressing the importance of AR and presenting awards for team and
individual successes.

Appoint a Change Agent. Another strategy involved the
Acquisition Reform Office itself. This group of experts served as
resources and facilitators for changes occurring throughout the system.
Because they worked hands-on with operations teams, they had the
opportunity to promulgate a wealth of information regarding both successes and lessons learned. They then disseminated this material
throughout the system. To help facilitate this exchange of information,
the office was supplemented by rotating professionals from the acquisition workforce, who served six to twelve months in this capacity before
returning to their regular jobs. Returning professionals continued to
engage in the reform work within their organizational "homes" while
staying linked to new information and tools coming out of the
Acquisition Reform Office. The team also included interns, executive
development program participants, and representatives from industry
and academia.

Link AR to Changes Across the System. Another strategy involved
identifying and taking advantage of opportunities for acquisition system
improvement. Surveys of the AR workforce during stand-downs have
provided tens of thousands of ideas. These recommendations are being
implemented by organizational, functional, and ad hoc teams that are
exploring better ways of doing business. In addition, the AR initiative
agenda was tied directly to congressional mandates and to the National
Performance Review, the organization founded by Vice President Al
Gore to "build a government that works better and costs less." This
alignment of AR with the goals and objectives of the executive branch
of the government has garnered increased support for AR initiatives.

Initiate a Continuous Dialogue with Industry. Senior Navy leaders
and the chief executive officers of the highest dollar contractors to the DoN
have met annually to focus on the changes under way and to discuss additional fixes needed to the acquisition system. At all levels, industry representatives participate in Integrated Product Teams (IPT), cross-functional
teams that manage a program throughout its life cycle. The IPT process
greatly facilitates communication among all acquisition personnel and

improves the quality of decision-making. Industry and government also partner to produce what are known as AR Roadshows. In these programs, organizations within certain geographical areas join with their industry counterparts to disseminate information about AR changes.

Remove Barriers. Changes in legislation and policy have made it easier to implement change and have opened communication among government organizations and between government employees and their industry counterparts. But, according to surveys of the acquisition workforce, the largest barrier to AR implementation is resistance to change. As shown in "Removing Barriers to Change," the more initiatives that are in progress, the lower people's receptivity to new initiatives and the lower the ability of the workforce to change (B4). However, as more successes are achieved, the system becomes more receptive to new initiatives, enhancing its ability to change and supporting the introduction of new initiatives (R5). Care must be taken not to add too many new initiatives, though, because overload could cause receptivity to fall again.

Deploy Innovations. The Acquisition Reform Office formalized a "Change Through Ex-Change" process to facilitate the dissemination of innovative ideas throughout the acquisition system. The process begins with a call to weapon systems programs to submit innovative ideas that they are implementing, that they feel will be successful, and that they think

REMOVING BARRIERS TO CHANGE

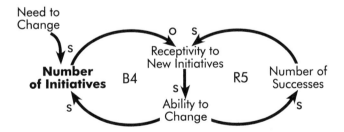

The more initiatives that are in progress, the lower people's receptivity to new initiatives and the lower the ability of the workforce to change (B4). However, as more successes are achieved, the system becomes more receptive to new initiatives, enhancing its ability to change and supporting the introduction of new initiatives (R5). Care must be taken not to add too many new initiatives, though, because overload could cause receptivity to fall again.

might be useful to other programs. These ideas are grouped into categories to facilitate ease of use and are listed on Internet and CD-ROM databases with search capabilities. In addition, the assistant secretary of the Navy (Research, Development, and Acquisition) hosts an annual conference to facilitate the exchange of ideas; the conference is attended by organizational representatives and "experts" on each innovation.

Communicate Widely. Both formal and informal vehicles for communication are important in an organization. Informal exchanges are stimulated by creating an environment that fosters open communication. An example in the DoN is the use of Integrated Product Teams and of Integrated Product and Process Development, a process and set of tools that promote concurrent development of weapon systems, thereby reducing cycle times for weapon development. The availability of information about successes promotes communication about different approaches in conferences, seminars, and informal exchanges.

The formal process of communication is both request-driven and event-driven. Request-driven ("pull") communications are reactive, resulting from actions initiated by stakeholders, such as congressional inquiries. The Acquisition Reform Home Page, which contains the latest information on implementation of AR in the Navy, is available for the stakeholder to access as needed. Videos and CD-ROMs are disseminated widely for lunch-time training and just-in-time use by workers.

Event-driven ("push") communications are proactive and are tied directly to the strategies for implementation of AR. The Acquisition Reform Office distributes newsletters and information alerts in hard copy, by email, and through the World Wide Web (www.acq-ref.navy.mil). Formal teams, such as the Acquisition Reform Team Working Group (ARTWG), have been established to facilitate the exchange of information. The ARTWG embodies the team-of-teams approach. Its members represent organizational and functional groups throughout the acquisition system. Each ARTWG team member has direct access to representatives of other acquisition teams throughout the United States. These representatives are responsible for disseminating information throughout their organizations.

For the last two years, the Navy has held a virtual town hall meeting. Through the use of real-time video teleconferencing, satellite downlink, television, Internet, video, telephone, and fax, the 40-plus members of the senior leadership team share information about future directions, discuss the latest changes, and answer questions from acquisition workers.

Acquisition Reform Offices have been established within the organization at the systems-command level to help facilitate the work of AR. These systems-command offices in turn facilitate initiatives in day-to-day operations. The AR team works with representatives from across the acquisition system to provide tools and support for process changes. These tools include information on successes and lessons learned to be used as benchmarks. Tools are widely distributed on CD-ROM and are available to both government and industry employees through the DoN Acquisition Reform Home Page.

Can You Move an Elephant?

Is Acquisition Reform changing the system? Coopers & Lybrand performed an external survey consisting of 430 structured interviews with 10 major Department of Defense contractors. These contractors are responsible for $17.4 billion worth of Department of Defense business. The study found that considerable progress has been achieved, while noting that there is still more to be accomplished. Looking internally, in comparing a May 1998 survey of the Department of the Navy acquisition workforce with similar surveys done in 1996 and 1997, it is clear that employees at every level see improvement in the acquisition process. Employees also feel that teams are improving the way they do their work. The foundation for this success was the recognition that communicating change is a systems problem and that many actions must be taken in parallel to ensure that "The Communication Success Loop" becomes a virtuous and not a vicious cycle. ⬿

Alex Bennet is an expert in communications and organizational change. She has an MS in management for organizational effectiveness and is currently pursuing her PhD in human and organizational systems. She is director of Communications, Education, and Training for Acquisition Reform and is part of the original Department of the Navy Acquisition Reform team.

Part Three

Transforming
People
and
Culture

In Part II, we read about some of the many different ways systems thinking and organizational learning tools and concepts can be used to tackle challenging issues. In this final section of the book, we "zoom in" closer than ever to see how four companies used organizational learning to address one particularly daunting challenge: reshaping their culture. Some of these companies framed their change effort in this way in order to restore their organization to health after a devastating decline in the company's fortunes. Others hoped to improve the knowledge base of their leadership or to heal a culture suffering from fear, mistrust, and uncertainty.

Part III offers stories from a rich blend of unique organizational cultures—from a not-for-profit enterprise to a technical college to a large, high-tech firm. Yet these stories transcend any surface-level differences. Reading them, we come to understand that reshaping culture has much more to do with people than with a company's particular setting or industry.

Using Organizational Learning Tools to Build Community

by James B. Rieley

The Milwaukee Area Technical College (MATC) is the largest two-year technical college in the U.S., serving nearly 70,000 students with an annual budget of over $203 million. Founded in 1912, the college was originally modeled after German trade schools, with an emphasis on factory-style efficiency. In addition, many of the college's senior administrators in the 1940s and 1950s had served as officers in World War II, giving the college a long history of military-style leadership and a command-and-control culture.

In 1982, however, a period of massive change began. The president of the college was forced to resign, and the college subsequently went through four presidents over a span of 13 years. After the most recent departure, an interim CEO was brought in to "clean up the mess" while the board of directors searched for yet another replacement.

Although the interim president was considered highly competent, he had a reputation for being more like Attila the Hun than Stephen Covey in terms of his leadership style. And despite the board's assurances that any interim replacement would not be eligible for the position, the acting president was eventually hired permanently. This decision, on top of years of change and instability, sent the organization into a state of shock. Daily rumors circulated about potential firings, and few people in the college felt secure enough to take risks. In order to regain our effectiveness as an organization, we needed to somehow work on rebuilding our community. But first, we needed to address the underlying issues that had bred a culture of fear and mistrust.

Examining the Culture

In September 1994, I discovered an article in *The Systems Thinker* Newsletter by Greg Zlevor entitled "Creating a New Workplace." The article asserted that all organizations operate at some point along a "community continuum": somewhere between "disciety" (dysfunctional society) and "community." It seemed to me that in order to improve our organizational climate, we first needed to identify where we were on the continuum. I shared the article with the director of research at MATC, and together we decided to conduct a "quick-and-dirty" survey based on Zlevor's model to get a sense of how our colleagues viewed our organization (see "MATC Community Survey"). Once it was complete, we mailed the survey to the entire management council of the college (more than 125 people).

To our surprise, we were inundated with phone calls the next morning. Many of the callers were struck by the candor of the statements, which were considered "undiscussables" in the organization. (The statements were taken verbatim from Zlevor's description of the different positions on the continuum.) Some callers had questions about confidentiality (their names were inadvertently included on the back of the survey, due to the internal mail routing labels). Several callers wanted to know if the new president was behind the survey. Still others were relieved that our organization was beginning to talk about these issues.

MATC COMMUNITY SURVEY

Please indicate, by checking the appropriate box, which statement best describes your perception of our current environment:

☐ This is war. Every person is for him- or herself.

☐ This place is so political. I see glimpses of kindness, but I usually feel beat up. I must protect myself.

☐ I do my part; they do theirs. As long as I keep to myself and do my job, I'm okay.

☐ People cooperate. We have our ups and downs, but mostly ups. There's a fair amount of trust. I can usually say what is on my mind. Everyone is important. Our differences make us better. We bring out the best in each other.

Amazingly, we received more than an 85 percent return rate on the surveys. We separated the responses into five piles, each representing a point along Zlevor's continuum. The results were almost perfectly bimodal: People saw the college as either dysfunctional ("This place is so political") or formative ("We have our ups and downs, but mostly ups"). We surmised that because there was no shared sense of the community as a whole, people's experience of the college depended to a large extent on the ups and downs of their daily experience.

We brought our data to the next meeting of the senior administrators (all of whom had received the survey) in order to explore the results. The dynamics of the ensuing discussion were as revealing as the survey results had been. Some people immediately demanded to know, "Why was my name put on the back of the survey!?" Others became defensive, wondering, "Why wasn't I told about the original article?" The group as a whole seemed to attack the validity of the survey itself, asking, "Why was this even done?" Their reactions seemed to reflect the overall climate of the organization—one of fear, mistrust, and well-entrenched defensive routines. At the conclusion of the meeting, they recommended that the entire survey episode be put to rest. However, it was not going to be forgotten that easily.

Reframing the Work

Earlier that year, a small group of people representing a cross-section of management had begun meeting regularly to learn more about systems thinking concepts and tools. The official title for the group was STOL—for Systems Thinking and Organizational Learning—but we jokingly referred to our get-togethers as "Systems Thinking over Lunch." Since our group had been using different case studies to hone our skills, I brought up the survey as a good opportunity to explore the larger dynamics at play in the organization. However, we quickly realized that the implications of this project were larger than any of our previous case studies—it really involved reframing how we thought about the nature of our entire organization.

As one of the ways to provide a framework for this effort, we decided to use the Vision Deployment Matrix™, a tool developed by Daniel Kim for helping groups articulate an action plan for moving from current reality toward a shared vision. The nine members of our STOL group filled out the Vision Deployment Matrix individually, then worked together to weave the individual perspectives into a collective matrix (see "MATC Vision Deployment Matrix"). After we filled out the first two vertical columns of the matrix—"Desired Future Reality" and "Current Reality"— we decided to get the president's input to see how his perceptions compared to our own.

After hearing a short explanation of the matrix, the president also filled out the first two columns. Interestingly, his responses were similar to ours. For example, in the box that indicated the systemic structures needed to achieve the vision, the STOL group had noted a need for "shared decision-making" and "effective communications," while the

MATC VISION DEPLOYMENT MATRIX

Level of Perspective	Desired Future Reality	Current Reality	Gaps or Challenges	Action Steps	Indicators of Progress
Vision MATC is committed to being a world-class educational institution that empowers students, faculty, and staff to realize their potential.	A place where we understand why we're here, where we're going, and what our collective values are and model them.	A distinct lack of collective values and alignment.			
Mental Models What are the beliefs and assumptions that will be congruent with the vision?	A belief that this environment is possible.	The system is too complex to be understood in an aligned fashion. Decisions are being made in a disjointed fashion with little or no feedback mechanism.			
Systemic Structures How can we create structures that will be consistent with those beliefs?	Clarity in both the decision parameters and processes, shared decision-making, and effective communications.	Emphasis on hierarchy, chain of command, lack of organizational accountability.			
Patterns What patterns of behavior do we want the structures to produce?	Risk-taking encouraged, successes celebrated, a "can-do" attitude modeled.	Cautious, insecure, not knowing.			
Events Can we describe tangible events that would indicate that the vision had been achieved?	Employees articulate and model the organizational vision.	People whisper and gossip instead of bringing issues into the open.			

To get a better picture of current reality at the college, and to paint a picture of the desired future, the STOL group used a tool called the Vision Deployment Matrix™. This diagram shows the collective responses of the STOL group to the first two columns of the matrix.

president expressed a desire for "more constructive meetings." This gave the STOL group confidence that the president shared our understanding of the vision and current reality of the college. In addition, his willingness to participate sent an important signal that he supported our efforts to examine and improve our organizational culture.

Improving Communication

Through the process of developing our matrix, we began to realize that one of our biggest obstacles to achieving our vision of improved community was the unspoken mental models held by members of the college—the untested assumptions that were preventing open and effective communication. This became clear at the next meeting of the Management Council, when the president gave a presentation on the issues facing the organization. After his talk, the STOL group then conducted a "left-hand column" exercise, in which the participants wrote down on the right side of the page what the president said, and on the left side voiced what they thought or felt in reaction to his comments.

What the group discovered through the process was that we all tend to hear what we expect to hear. For example, the people who anticipated hearing only "bad news" heard precisely that. Those who expected to see a

---

The left-hand column exercise opened up our awareness of the significant role our mental models play in selecting what we hear and don't hear.

"tough guy" in the president had their predictions confirmed. And, intriguingly, the people who were open to organizational change saw the shifts that were occurring as a positive development for the college (see "Left-Hand Column: One Perspective" on p. 122 for an example of this exercise). This exercise opened up our awareness of the significant role our mental models play in selecting what we hear and don't hear, and it had the desired effect of opening the group up to a deeper level of conversation. Our work in developing a deeper level of community was beginning to take hold.

LEFT-HAND COLUMN: ONE PERSPECTIVE

What I Am Thinking	What Was Said
If things are clear, why wouldn't people understand? If we ask questions, we will look stupid, or be made to feel stupid.	"You need to ask questions if you don't understand."
His positive examples referenced "he," not "we." Aren't we all in this together?	"We need to continue despite obstacles."
We **are** *all in this together.*	"I am struggling with all of this stuff. It is hard work, but important."
What does he mean—positions, persons, or just putting the issue "on hold," waiting for reorganization?	"There will be no loss in positions."
Some of the "issues to be resolved" were obviously decisions that have already been made. What happened to shared decision-making and communication before announcements?	"Here are some policy issues that need to be resolved."

After a talk by the president to the Management Council, the STOL group conducted a "left-hand column" exercise, in order to surface the mental models operating in the group.

Preliminary Results

When the STOL group developed its Vision Deployment Matrix, we noted that one of the indicators of progress toward developing community would be an openness in communication throughout the administration of the college, as well as an increased ability as a group to suspend our assumptions and inquire more deeply into each other's reasoning. The area where we have seen the greatest progress toward this goal has been in the Management Council meetings. In the past, they were full-day sessions that consisted primarily of lectures given by the president and/or his direct reports. The attendees often felt "talked at" for hours on end. There was very little participation, and many attendees passed the time by surreptitiously doing paperwork. When we did a quick analysis of the cost of the meetings, we discovered that the college was spending approximately $100,000 per year on a function that yielded very little benefit.

We decided, therefore, to use the Management Council meetings as an opportunity to work on developing better communication, and to begin to tap into the collective intelligence of the members. We shortened the meetings to half-day sessions, eliminated the speakers, and refocused the agenda on working together in small groups to tackle some of the serious issues facing our institution. At the first of the re-designed management meetings, two college-wide issues that were generally considered to be undiscussables were addressed:

(1) how to better implement the entire Continuous Quality Improvement process; and

(2) how to productively examine the positive and negative effects of the changes that occurred within the organization during the last several years.

In order to facilitate more productive communication at the meeting, we assigned people to small groups, each of which represented a cross-section of the college. As the groups were invited to share their insights with the entire council, previously undiscussable issues were surfaced, and some very productive conversations ensued. For example, the "undiscussable" issue of a compensation and benefits inequity between union and non-union employees was raised, and specific recommendations were made for further action. After the meeting, we shared the outputs with the president (who chose not to be present during the meeting so as not to inhibit open communication), and we forwarded the results to the CQI Steering Committee of the college.

Our Ongoing Work

The evaluations from our first redesigned Management Council meeting were very positive. Many people commented that the college was "finally moving forward." But even as we celebrated this modest success, we recognized that we had a long way to go toward our goal of developing a healthy community at MATC. In order to continue work on organizational integration and community building, the STOL group identified four areas for further action:

- continue to work on building communication and trust;

- make systems thinking courses and materials available to others at the college;
- continue to develop systemic solutions for problems at the college, working with the president to effect high-leverage changes;
- re-survey the Management Council to accurately assess current reality at the college.

As we further developed our skills in community building and in creating structures to sustain that community, we looked ahead to making a profound difference in the organizational culture. With the help of organizational learning tools, we felt confident that our culture would continue to move toward openness and community. ⌐

James B. Rieley directed the Center for Continuous Quality Improvement at MATC. Currently, he is a manager of the Knowledge Services Competency Center in Arthur Andersen's Business Consulting division in Houston, where he works to facilitate effective organizational change.

Individual and Team Empowerment: Human Dynamics at Digital

by Chris Strutt

The meeting was in full swing. Key players from management, technical leadership, engineering, and marketing had assembled to discuss several critical strategic product decisions. But as the meeting progressed, a serious disagreement emerged between a technical leader and a business manager.

Both people were convinced that their perspective was right. The technical leader was focused on the longer term—what he knew could be done to delight the customer 12 months down the road. The business manager, on the other hand, was focused on the customers' present needs. She wanted the team to look at the problems that needed to be solved in the next product release, due out in three months. The argument escalated until the two were shouting at each other across the table.

Although it appeared that the two perspectives were in opposition, the truth was that both people were in violent agreement on the underlying value of meeting the customer's needs. Their conflict was due to fundamental distinctions in the way they thought about, processed, and perceived the world. The technical leader was focused on the longer-term vision, while the business manager was focused on the next practical step—both equally important and valuable perspectives that held the customer as the number-one priority.

Fortunately, another team member noticed this distinction and explained what was happening. He pointed out how their different personality dynamics were leading to this disconnect, and that they really were on the same track in many ways. The two players both stopped in silence, suddenly realizing how they were caught up in their own perspectives. Meanwhile, another engineer, expressing his characteristic gift of empathy, admitted, "And I *feel* your pain!" Everyone in the room broke up with laughter, releasing the tension that they, too, felt. The group was then able to move on and develop some productive solutions that would serve the customers' long-term needs, while still addressing the immediate issues that needed to be resolved.

Human Dynamics

This incident, which took place within the former Digital's Networks Software Group, is an example of how many people are beginning to apply a fundamental new understanding about how human beings function, called Human Dynamics™. This technology has been researched and developed by Dr. Sandra Seagal since 1979, and it offers a framework for understanding differences in the way people learn, communicate, relate, and develop as human beings. Human Dynamics presents a systemic approach to the complexities and wonders of human functioning that is clear, logical, and structured, yet broad and flexible enough to encompass the infinite nuances that make each of us unique human beings (see "Human Dynamics: An Overview").

Human Dynamics was introduced into Digital Equipment Corporation in 1993 and became a central part of everyday functioning for people in many groups across the organization. Some said it became as fundamental as knowing the alphabet—so much a part of the way they thought and communicated that they took it for granted.

The Beginning

It all began in August 1992, when the Networks Group recognized that Human Dynamics was a critical technology that could enhance and leverage Digital's efforts to return to profitability. That was also the beginning of two years of restructuring, downsizing, and cost containment, which was the mandate if we were to survive as a viable company.

As the company launched itself into that difficult work, our concern was, "What are we doing for the survivors?" Research statistics on large

HUMAN DYNAMICS: AN OVERVIEW

The following is an excerpt from "Human Dynamics: A Foundation for the Learning Organization," by Sandra Seagal and David Horne, which originally appeared in the May, 1994, issue of *The Systems Thinker*™:

Human Dynamics explores the interaction of three universal principles: the mental, the emotional (or relational), and the physical (or practical). The mental principle is related to the mind—to thinking, values, structure, focus, objectivity, and perspective. The emotional principle is concerned with relationships—with communication, organization, feelings, and putting things together in new ways (creativity). The physical principle is pragmatic—it is the making, doing, and operationalizing part of ourselves.

These three principles combine in nine possible variations to form distinct ways of functioning, which are termed "personality dynamics." Each constitutes a whole way of functioning, characterized by distinct processes of learning, communicating, problem-solving, relating to others, contributing to teams, maintaining well-being, and responding to stress. The personality dynamics appear in every culture, characterize males and females equally, and can be observed at every age level.

It is essential to understand that Human Dynamics is a developmental paradigm. A person's dynamic remains consistent over time, but is expressed with increasing maturity. Maturation involves the integration and development of the mental, emotional, and physical aspects of each personality dynamic.

corporations who downsize clearly show that only a fraction of them actually return to profitability—and an even smaller fraction return to previous levels of employee productivity and morale. From our prior work with systems thinking and learning skills, we knew that the most fundamental obstacle to improved product quality and customer satisfaction—and hence profitability—lay in the absence, avoidance, or breakdown of authentic communication between human beings.

Our work in Human Dynamics initially started as a "grass-roots" effort. Funds were "tin-cupped" from five concerned middle managers and used to train two people to become licensed Human Dynamics facilitators. When they returned from their training, the two facilitators could hardly stop talking about the power of Human Dynamics to help build team synergy and productivity. Soon the first formal request for a workshop came in. In May 1993 this workshop was delivered, and it received an evaluation of 5.5 on a 6-point scale.

That same month, Sandra Seagal and David Horne came to Digital in Littleton, Massachusetts, and delivered a workshop for the Networks

Group vice president and his newly forming leadership team. As a result of this experience, the team was able to recognize, understand, and appreciate the special gifts that each of them brought to their work—knowledge they used over the next several months as they established Digital's core Networking Business.

A Boost in the Middle

From initial experiences like these, word of the power and usefulness of Human Dynamics soon spread. For example, a program manager needed some critical decisions to be made by a technical leader. She knew her own personality dynamic and his, and she was aware of the distinctions and potential points of conflict in their communication processes: She would naturally approach the issue by building up from the details until the structure emerged, whereas he would identify the principles and structure first, and then fill in the details. Knowing this, she designed her communication to best suit his process, by starting with the structure first. As a result, they secured the required decision in one 15-minute conversation. Prior to her understanding of the significance of personality dynamics, the same issue would have been addressed through multiple two-hour arguments and discussions. While the result might have been the same, the cost—in terms of time, energy, and goodwill—would have been much greater.

Such anecdotes drew the attention of the late Peter Conklin, who was then serving as leader of the Engineering Excellence Program. He saw the importance of this work in engineering, where teams deal with increasingly complex issues that require the clearest possible communication to make rapid decisions that are also sustainable. So, in January 1994, Peter funded the training of four new facilitators—and Human Dynamics became an official educational program under the auspices of Digital's Engineering Excellence Program.

Over the next four months, we began offering four to five workshops per month, each one jointly facilitated by two of our Human Dynamics facilitators. Workshops were delivered to "intact" teams who focused on delivering a product, service, or specific set of results. These teams usually spanned organizational, functional, and hierarchical boundaries.

We were very encouraged by the ongoing requests for workshops. Our past experience showed that the best indicator for the value or usefulness of any new technology is the level of continued demand. Since the Human Dynamics work began as a bottom-up effort and continued as a middle-across effort through the Engineering Excellence program, we knew that no one was seeking a workshop just because he or she was being pressured by upper management.

Naturally, there were people who were somewhat skeptical of what they saw as another "team-building" workshop. Engineers in particular

---

The vast majority of skeptics saw the practical value of Human Dynamics by the end of the first day of training.

(who made up about half of the participants) were very wary of what they called "touchy-feely" stuff. The vast majority of these skeptics, however, saw the practical value of Human Dynamics by the end of the first day of training. This was in large part due to the open, interactive process of the workshop, and the fact that it centered on self-identification. In addition, people seemed to appreciate the holistic nature of the Human Dynamics technology, along with its recognition of each individual's intrinsic value and infinite developmental capacity.

A few people (about 3 percent) continued to be skeptical, even after the training, because of their fundamental objection to any form of categorization or "labeling," as they saw it. These negative reactions were rooted in past experiences with traditional typologies, where people were not only categorized by an "expert," but they often felt judged as being of lesser value than other types. There is no such value judgment inherent in the Human Dynamics work, but it clearly remains a concern for some people.

A Setback

While the groundwork in Human Dynamics was being laid, Digital was still struggling to get back on its feet financially. The quarter ending in December 1993 was a profitable one—the first in a very long while. It felt good, but many of us were afraid that it was only a "blip" on the screen due to short-term actions and symptomatic fixes. As it turned out, the company was seriously back in the red the following quarter. As a result, starting in May 1994, the company underwent the most severe belt-tightening yet. Among many things, this included an immediate stop to most training expenses. Overnight, the Human Dynamics program came to a halt. Even worse, five of our six Human Dynamics facilitators left the company as a result of cutbacks in overhead functions.

Yet although no new people were being trained in Human Dynamics, those who had been trained continued to use their understandings to work more effectively. One group vice president faced a reporting structure above her that changed four times during this period. Fortunately, she knew her own personality dynamic and that of each new manager. From her Human Dynamics training, she understood what this meant in terms of differences in communication preferences, and the way they each approached problem solving and decision-making. So she used her understanding to tailor her communication to each person, consciously using the most helpful language for that individual. As a result, she continued to get much of the support she needed for the success of her business, despite the many changes in the hierarchy above her.

Many of us using Human Dynamics at Digital continued to deepen our understanding of the methodology through tutorials and lunchtime, "brown-bag" seminars. The aim was to share our actual experiences with Human Dynamics and to coach people in its everyday application. By this time, we were using Human Dynamics as a kind of short-hand that alerted us to listen more effectively to each other by understanding the special gifts and perspectives that each of us brings.

By late 1994, the company was finishing the final stages of its restructuring, and it was settling down to about 60,000 employees world-wide— half its original size. The moratorium on training expenses began to lighten. After a seven-month hiatus, a Human Dynamics workshop was delivered in December 1994. As before, word quickly spread and more requests followed.

Margaret Ledger, the new manager of Digital's Technical Competency Development Group (TCDG), began to see Human Dynamics as a foundational technology for effective project team leadership and operation across the company. With support from key people in the newly formed business segments, including Peter Conklin and Jean

Proulx, Margaret incorporated Human Dynamics into the TCDG's core curriculum, to be delivered on demand across the company. Once again, Human Dynamics was formally embedded in a "middle-across" program, this time alongside the delivery of technical training such as C++, Object Oriented Design, and Windows 95.

Sustainment

During 1995, Human Dynamics reached almost 600 people across the company, and the demand for more workshops remained steady. In April 1995, three new facilitators were trained.

A key challenge facing the company was to establish more frequent and regular mechanisms for sharing experiences and offering "refresher" seminars. Also, we still had to learn how to surface the really difficult "undiscussables" that Chris Argyris has talked about. But we knew that Human Dynamics had given us an immensely valuable springboard from which to begin this work.

Sustaining this kind of forward momentum in any company requires the continued empowerment, connection, and creative potential of each and every employee. Human Dynamics, which goes to the very core of human functioning and development, can serve as a foundational technology toward these ends.

Epilogue

In early 1998, Digital Equipment Corporation was acquired by Compaq Computers. What does this mean for the Human Dynamics learnings that had taken place in earlier years at Digital? Since Compaq's acquisition, Human Dynamics workshops are still offered as part of the Technical Competency Development Program curriculum. Compaq is now in the midst of major restructuring, including plans to lay off 15,000 people, so very little training is being delivered at this time. However, the Digital experience has left several important legacies.

Most importantly, Digital was the first large, high-tech corporation to utilize Human Dynamics to improve bottom-line business results in a systemic way. As such, the company served as a "stepping stone" or "practice field" for other large, high-tech companies such as Intel, who are now reaping even more widespread results with Human Dynamics.

Secondly, products developed within Digital by project teams consciously applying their Human Dynamic learnings continue to generate revenues for Compaq. These products include industry-award-winning Internet collaboration software.

Thirdly, because the technology is so powerfully awakening for people, employees across the company continue to use their Human Dynamics understandings to enhance everyday interactions. In addition, as Digital shrank from 120,000 to 60,000 employees during its final years of existence, many of those departing have gone on to share the benefits of Human Dynamics with colleagues at other companies, as well as with their families and communities. For example, at Security Dynamics Technologies Inc. and at RSA Inc., both industry leaders in security technology, Human Dynamics has been introduced to several engineering and marketing teams, with immediate and good results. ✑

Chris Strutt concluded 24 years service at Digital in January 1997 and now works as an independent consultant, coach, and facilitator. She helps people in all walks of life to connect deeply with themselves and with each other, enabling their unique gifts and highest potential to be fully appreciated and engaged in producing whatever results are needed in the world. She divides her time between business applications for team effectiveness; applications in schools with educators, parents, and children; and applications in the community for diversity awareness and the improvement of relationships of all kinds. Chris is also engaged in projects that nurture the awakening of authentic leadership in all individuals and the emergence of spiritual purpose at work.

Chapter Fifteen

Connecting the Heart and Mind at EDS

by Francine Zucker

In May 1994, I was asked to lead a team of marketing communications professionals within EDS, a Fortune 100 professional services company in the global information technology industry. This highly talented group of graphic artists, writers, and marketing people was in turmoil. The emotional climate in the department was characterized by fear, distrust, and a lack of respect for colleagues and management. Serious performance problems had begun to crop up.

About the same time, I became aware of a movement within EDS to adopt the management philosophies of the learning organization. I participated in an extensive program within EDS on the use of organizational learning concepts and introduced those principles to my team (see "Learning Peaks and Valleys" on p. 134). Now, three years later, we are no longer just a "graphics production shop"; we have expanded this view and have transformed ourselves into a full-service resource for integrated marketing communications for EDS's Eastern Region offices and its government business worldwide. This achievement represents a paradigm shift for our team and for the other departments with which we work.

A key insight contributed to this shift: that sustained learning requires recognizing emotions as integral to human interactions and performance in the workplace. This acknowledgment was our first step in understanding the "emotional landscape" of our team. Emotional landscape is the mood, sense, or feel of the organization based on individual experiences and perceptions. Why is this understanding important?

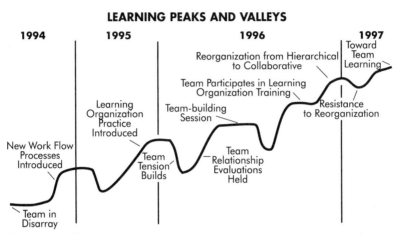

LEARNING PEAKS AND VALLEYS

This graphic illustrates the team's continuing journey in creating sustained team learning and a shared vision. Learning occurred at each peak and valley.

Because emotions bring the passion, excitement, energy, and drive that fuel commitment to a shared vision and produce results toward achieving that vision.

We have found a place for the constructive expression of emotions in a work setting. Because people are not used to expressing feelings in the workplace, we must learn how to bring the full range of human emotions into our work lives. We call this process "developing emotional competency." Thus, our journey toward team learning has involved integrating feeling with intellect, balancing emotions with logic, and connecting the heart and mind in the workplace.

Operating "From the Neck Up"

The strategic marketing communications function within EDS includes planning and developing marketing campaigns, advertisements, and other promotional materials to support EDS's Eastern Region business, primarily in the government market. Much like an advertising agency, we develop and present creative concepts to management; we operate under tight deadlines; and we are continually under pressure to generate new ideas.

During my first year with the group, our workload reached an overwhelming volume, and our ability to function as a team had begun to decline. We missed deadlines; our design concepts were off the mark; relationships with colleagues outside our team were poor; and there was ongoing tension among team members. We developed new processes and procedures to fix our production problems, but soon realized that rules and schedules by themselves cannot create a team learning environment. Although we achieved some improvements, our problems persisted, and we felt tempted to blame everyone else for these difficulties.

By exploring the organizational learning disciplines, we identified a fundamental learning disability: People operate "from the neck up" in the workplace. They think and act mostly from their heads, which may be out of step with their hearts. This imbalance can ultimately contribute to dysfunctional business relationships. If people do not feel free to express the emotions that surround their work, whether pride, humor,

---

We identified a fundamental learning disability: People operate "from the neck up" in the workplace.

---

joy, frustration, fear, sadness, or anger, they are not bringing their whole selves to their work. As a result, the team does not experience the full creative force of the individuals in it. During our team's early struggles, we were becoming apathetic and compliant, as opposed to committed and passionate about our work. Clearly, we needed to create a more supportive environment where people could constructively express their emotions surrounding their work.

Creating a Supportive Environment

While working to surface the undercurrent of unexpressed emotions in our environment, we acknowledged the need to improve team members' relationships with one another. We also recognized that we had to develop the interpersonal skills critical to team building, such as trust, respect, accountability, emotional bonds, and information sharing. At one difficult but critical turning point, we participated in an extensive team-relationship evaluation, in which each person evaluated every member of the team. Team members filled out written evaluation forms to address key relationship issues surrounding team building. For example, members were asked to comment on an individual's ability to build relationships based on trust, tolerance, and respect. Each person was asked to respond anonymously and not to discuss the evaluations.

I then met with each person individually to review the comments made by his or her peers. We also met as a team to discuss the feelings surrounding the process and what each person learned from the experience. Team members shared what they understood to be their strengths and weaknesses, and made a six-month commitment to improve in a specific area. One person pledged to listen more closely to team members. Another made a commitment to become more involved in team projects. Individuals performed the evaluations honestly and maturely, and the process, though challenging, brought us closer together as a team. We continued to renew our commitments every six months.

The team-relationship evaluations were the catalyst we needed to identify our learning disabilities and address the unexpressed emotions that were creating problems. From there, we instituted methods that became part of our daily work lives, including:

- *Practicing authentic communication*, which means identifying concerns and coming forward with the thoughts and feelings surrounding them. For example, "You missed the deadline, and now I have less time to do my part of the project. I feel angry because I have to rush, and I feel hurt because you don't respect my time." We found that addressing these difficult issues immediately is the best way to develop emotional competency.
- *Instituting a check-in process* at the beginning of our Monday morning business meetings. We started with an insightful or inspirational story. Each team member then had an opportunity to share a feeling, reflect on past work, give his or her thoughts about the week ahead, or simply pass. The check-in enables team members to express their concerns and joys.
- *Continuing to recognize people's work*. For example, we regularly honored individuals with small gifts (requiring more thought than money) to recognize performance. We provided monetary rewards for outstanding achievement and sent letters to the company's executive leadership about our team's efforts.

Our experience with organizational learning confirmed the need to create an environment where individuals can express their thoughts and feelings. In this atmosphere, our team grew more confident, motivated, energetic, and creative.

Revealing Team Mental Models

In addition to changing some of our regular practices, we also concluded that some of the mental models we held about our work were interfering with the team's performance. We identified several of these:

- *"Only designers have creative ideas."* Many team members would defer creative decisions to the designers because "that's their job," instead of working more collaboratively. When people work collaboratively, everyone is considered a source of creativity and feels a sense of responsibility to contribute to a design concept.

- *"It's us versus them."* We saw "them" as the internal organizations we supported, such as our marketing communications colleagues. In fact, it took two years for us to view them as our colleagues, not as our customers or enemies. We shifted our view to focus on what we could learn from them, what value they offered, and how their work contributed to the larger goal. This new way of thinking came to be known in our team as "getting big."

- *"Our value is less than an ad agency; that's why we work for a corporation."* Some team members felt that our function in the corporation was "less than" that of other groups, and that we, as individuals, were not as creative as the people who work for advertising agencies. This perception was often reinforced by other internal groups who contracted work out to agencies to get "better creative ideas."

- By far, the most debilitating team mental model was the idea that *"we are just a production shop."* This statement implies an assembly-line approach to graphic design, with little regard for strategy, the creative process, or the corporate vision. We challenged this mental model by changing the process by which we accepted and managed projects, and by creating new roles within the team to focus on strategy, corporate direction, and new business development. We contracted out some production services to free up team members to focus on communications strategies and large-scale government marketing programs. As a result, we turned what was once our most dysfunctional mental model into our shared vision. We elevated our role and became a resource for strategic marketing communications across the region.

This transformation was never more evident than on a subsequent project to promote EDS's government business. The project was multifaceted, complex, global in scope, and on a tight schedule. Because of our team's new, strategic shared vision and greater confidence in our capabilities, we turned what could have been a series of disjointed communications projects into an integrated marketing communications program with a cohesive theme, a clear direction, and a global reach.

Although the results of this project were quite positive, the journey was stormy. Time constraints and the pressures of a high-profile project brought out old patterns of behavior. In the past, these behaviors would have had a negative effect on the project. Yet, as one team member said, "We're still here and we're still talking with each other." We could not have succeeded as a team on this kind of project without the practice in emotional competency.

Instituting Reinforcing Structures

To continue this work and bring it more fully into our daily work life, we developed ways to reinforce our practice. For example:

- We reengineered the organization to be less structured and less hierarchical than it had been. The new organization now promotes shared accountability and shared learning. We respect and value everyone's contribution and have eliminated the mental model, "only designers have creative ideas."

- We began holding quarterly, off-site team meetings to reflect on how we were growing as an organization and where we wanted to go. Each meeting incorporated a component of team learning, such as developing personal mission statements, which demonstrate how each individual contributes to the larger whole.

- We held spontaneous team meetings, when necessary, to address issues "in the moment," and to discuss feelings that impact our working relationships.

- We made a commitment to educate ourselves about leading-edge marketing communications strategies that will take our work to a new level of quality.

- We also made a commitment to build awareness internally and externally of the quality of the strategies and materials we produce. With this renewed confidence in our creative talents, we made great strides in debunking the perception that "our value is less than an ad agency," or that "we are just a production shop."

Business Benefits and Learnings

The greatest business benefit of our change work was that our team became more cohesive and functioned at a higher level of performance than before. Quality, productivity, and creativity have all flourished in this environment. Individuals can see their role in the organization more clearly. They have a better sense of "the big picture" and know that what they do makes a difference. Communicating more openly and being aware of the emotional undercurrents in our daily work life have greatly improved relationships among team members, management, and the groups we support.

As a result, we have become more focused and efficient than ever in the delivery of our services. We have been able to work more col-

Combining the disciplines of organizational learning with the practice of constructively expressing emotions was the foundation of our work in becoming a learning organization.

laboratively with various organizations. And, we have broadened our ability to service additional areas of EDS's Eastern Region business. We now have more confidence and have made numerous contributions to all levels of government marketing and communications.

Combining the disciplines of organizational learning with the practice of constructively expressing emotions is the foundation of our work in becoming a learning organization. We've learned that building and maintaining a learning community requires a concerted effort to bring the heart and mind together in the workplace, and we believe this practice is the key to sustaining business success.

Epilogue

I left EDS's Eastern Region Marketing Communications Division in early 1998. Since that time, I've reflected a bit on the division's experience with organizational learning, and on how things have evolved over this year.

Several important lessons stand out in my mind. The biggest insight, in my opinion, is that to sustain organizational learning within a hierarchical organization like EDS requires the commitment of midlevel managers and team leaders. This reality stems from several factors; namely, the impact of turnover in such organizations, the lack of coaching and internal change agents, and the tendency to drop the so-called "soft" skills during times of change and crisis.

Specifically, if a new leader comes in who doesn't support an established learning effort, then the effort will likely evaporate. Despite my efforts to prepare the team for the change in leadership, team learning processes were not sustained by the new leader. Moreover, of the 15 people who made up the marketing communications division, only four remain.

This turnover rate underscores the need for consistent, committed leadership in sustaining communities of commitment. Within hierarchical organizations, there is more of a burden on team leaders to provide the steady, consistent encouragement of team learning efforts. Building a culture that embraces organizational learning takes immense work and commitment. Unfortunately, at times, many of the principles and skills that characterize organizational learning are considered "soft" by upper management. During times of corporate change or crisis, investment in and attention to team learning are often dropped, thus placing the burden on midlevel managers and their team leaders to sustain organizational learning efforts.

Management at the executive level leads the way for organizational learning. However, I am more convinced than ever that it's the midlevel managers and team leaders who are the foundation for sustaining communities of commitment. Simply put, these people are essential to the longevity and practice of team learning. ᕦ

Francine Zucker served as regional manager for Marketing Communications at EDS. As a leader in organizational learning, Ms. Zucker has published *Connecting the Heart and Mind at Work: A Leader's Guide*.

Editorial assistance for this chapter was provided by Patti Cochrano.

Chapter Sixteen

Toward a New Culture: The Power of Aligning with Deep Purpose

by Sharon Lehrer

How does an organization tap into its sense of purpose to effect enduring change? In 1995, the Institute of Noetic Sciences embarked on a journey of change that would dramatically transform its culture. The process involved strikingly innovative practices, and the journey proved far more challenging and rewarding than the organization could have imagined. During this time, the organization turned inward to reflect on its own sense of meaning, to practice the very ideas they had been promoting to others for 23 years, and to challenge long-held mental models. In the end, this soul searching led not only to a new purpose and vision, but also to a transformation of the culture and the development of new leadership capacities.

About the Institute

The Institute of Noetic[1] Sciences (IONS) is a not-for-profit organization that was founded in 1973 for the purpose of conducting research into consciousness and human potential and its implications for global mind change. Its explorations encompass such phenomena as mind-body healing, the role of intentionality in influencing physical reality, expanded perceptual capacities, the power of belief systems, and nonrational ways of knowing. IONS is funded by contributions from its 50,000 members and other donors.

[1] The word *noetic* comes from the Greek word *nous*, which means mind, or ways of knowing. Noetic science is concerned with subjective experience, holistic modes of perception, values, and understanding, and complements the prediction and control models that form the bases of mainstream Western science.

Over the years, IONS grew to a staff of about 35 and succeeded in conveying its research findings to its members and the public through publications and educational forums. Yet the organization had rarely applied noetic ideas to its own internal processes of strategic management. Nor had it invested in the best practices from organizational development (OD), such as the use of consultants, offsite retreats, or training for team and leadership development.

Early Thinking About Change

In 1994, the organization clarified its thinking about organizational learning when it stated, "We aim at being a team in which all share in the creation of our guiding vision, and in the commitment to the highest level of individual and group performance; in which we all learn together; and in which our central purpose is achieving our own fulfillment through serving the whole." This statement helped set the context for the change initiative that followed a year later.

By 1995 it was clear that many other institutions besides IONS were conducting similar research and producing similar publications. Yet it took the "fresh eyes" of a new member of IONS' board of directors to identify the need to redefine IONS' purpose, mission, organizational practices, and leadership to prepare for the 21st century. Thus IONS decided to launch a major strategic planning effort to reassess, renew, and refound the Institute.

The initial approach to the change initiative was fairly conventional. The board expected a well-designed and controlled planning process, a strategic plan that would provide answers and solutions, and completion in two years. Yet they knew on some level that in order to create a new vision, the organization would have to break out of its existing organizational paradigm. Was it willing to question its core beliefs? Was it willing to use multiple ways of knowing for planning, visioning, and decision-making?

Preparing for the Journey: Guiding Questions

During a series of retreats, staff meetings, informal conversations, and individual reflections, two primary questions about purpose emerged that would inform IONS' strategic planning process for the next two-and-a-half years:

1. What is IONS' deepest calling?
2. What is my [each staff and board member's] deepest purpose as it relates to IONS?

Using Noetic Ideas to Transform Culture

Winston ("Wink") Franklin, the CEO of IONS, was influenced by the work of David Bohm, and Margaret Wheatley and Myron Kellner-Rogers. Bohm, the eminent quantum physicist, had devoted much of his later life to studying the nature of shared meaning, purposeful coherence, and collective consciousness. Wheatley's and Kellner-Rogers' ideas about organizations as living systems with the capacity for self-organization and life as a self-organizing system were familiar to many in the organization.

Bohm's, Wheatley's, and Kellner-Rogers' work informed the processes and practices that IONS began to use in its change initiative. These practices, which differ markedly from traditional OD methods, were introduced by Wink and myself and captured the imagination of many at IONS. Indeed, the adoption of such practices became a prominent theme in IONS' change effort.

Embracing the Noetic: The Board of Directors

At the board of directors' retreat, the group used a blend of intuitive processes to explore the two core questions about purpose. One exercise included board members' spending six hours in silence—walking in nature, writing in journals, and reflecting alone, as well as eating together.

Later in the exercise, after meditating and engaging in sacred chanting together, each board member drew a mandala. A mandala is a sacred circle representing our wholeness and interdependence with the universe, and is common in Tibetan, Hindu, Native American, and other spiritual traditions (see "A Sacred Mandala" on p. 144).

Inside the mandala circle, participants drew symbols such as a flower, a sun, mountains, or a shooting star. Next, they added words that illuminated their personal purpose as it related to IONS. Finally, they reflected on the common themes that emerged in the mandalas.

For example, one person drew a simple house with grass, flowers, and animals all around. To him, this represented his purpose to create a safe, nourishing home (organization) with all the necessary resources in order to explore frontier noetic ideas. Later, each person's mandala was placed

A SACRED MANDALA

A mandala is a sacred circle representing our wholeness and interdependence with the universe.

Source: Marion Weber

on a large "Board Mandala" so that everyone could see his or her unique contribution to the whole. Combining the individual mandalas in this way also helped the group hold the intention behind IONS' planning process and change initiative.

Through such exercises, the board members tapped into their collective wisdom, gaining insights and information they could not have accessed through rational means alone.

A remarkable thing happened as a result of this activity: The board changed the name of their process from "Strategic Planning" to "Inspired Inquiry and Visionary Planning." They had decided that they wanted to dream, imagine, and tap their intuition, and to experiment

> *Through such exercises, the board members tapped into their collective wisdom, gaining insights and information they could not have accessed through rational means alone.*

with new methods to shape IONS' future, *before* they engaged in strategic considerations. Their use of nontraditional methods proved a major turning point in IONS' approach to strategic planning and marked the emergence of a noetic model for organizational planning. As one board member said, "Perhaps our most important contribution will be our process—how we live 'noetically' with each other as a community and in our lives." Through these courageous decisions to experiment with noetic processes, the change initiative embodied the organization's new purpose and vision—not only to research and educate others about noetic sciences, but to "live" them as well.

Developing Shared Leadership: The Story of the HOT Team

Like the board of directors, midlevel managers at IONS were eager to apply noetic approaches to their work as well. Within the first few months of the change initiative, Wink established a cross-departmental team to develop better ways for IONS to serve its most active members. From the very first, this team became self-organizing and took on a life of its own. Members named the team "the Heart of Transformation" (HOT).

The HOT team decided early on to experiment with multiple ways of knowing and learning. One remarkable achievement that emerged out of the way the team functioned was a new governance model—that of shared leadership. The very nature of the practices the HOT team used encouraged the sharing of leadership within the team. For example, a key leadership skill is knowing how to create a safe "container" for meetings—one that encourages all participants to share their wisdom and play a leadership role, and one free from fear, competition, and judgment. The HOT team created this "container" through several innovative means drawn from IONS' research in the noetic realm:

Check-Ins. A practice known as check-in became an integral part of the HOT team's meetings. Check-ins are modeled after the talking circles used by indigenous peoples and after what Bohm called dialogue, a process for sharing from the heart, learning from others, observing one's assumptions, and making decisions. Conducted in a circle without a leader, check-ins allow everyone to speak, give equal weight to each person's comments, and encourage respectful listening. The practice also makes the group's collective wisdom visible to the participants.

Often, what emerged during a HOT team check-in would inform the rest of the meeting. For example, the group might decide that their original agenda for the meeting was no longer relevant, and would change it to address issues that had arisen during the check-in. Over time, the group discovered that their real business was reflected most vividly in the passion of the group members' ideas and emotions. Check-ins became a way to harness this passion and use it to fulfill the team's mission.

Transformative Storytelling. As the culture at IONS gradually began shifting, change often disrupted the collective psyche and personal lives of the people involved. HOT team meetings offered a safe place to speak about these transitions. During meetings, participants often experienced healing, transformation, and a sense of compassion for one another through the telling of personal stories. As one HOT team member explained, "We gained an appreciation for the diversity of tasks that are handled here at IONS. I went about my own job and didn't realize that others had deadlines and different things to accomplish. By listening to people's stories, I realized that even though we are all in different places in the organization, we are very similar."

Sometimes just telling one's story and being heard proved healing. At other times, a personal story helped clarify an organizationwide issue. For example, during one meeting the team realized that one woman's personal story about a death in her family paralleled the dying of old beliefs and patterns of behavior at IONS. The sadness and grief for the woman's loss

---

Even though many people at IONS wanted to let go of such beliefs, there was resistance and fear as well. As people connected to these feelings, they began exploring these beliefs, and new ways of being began to emerge.

---

evoked similar feelings in the group about what was happening at IONS. Letting go of longstanding mental models was painful. For example, deep beliefs about the superiority of the intellect over other ways of knowing, and of male leadership over female leadership, were embedded not only in IONS' paradigm but are firmly anchored in Western culture as well. Even though many people at IONS wanted to let go of such beliefs, there was resistance and fear as well. As people connected to these feelings, they began exploring these beliefs, and new ways of being began to emerge. Bringing emotions into the open and naming them relieved staff members' feelings of isolation and helped them actively address underlying dynamics at IONS.

Guided Imagery. The HOT team also used guided imagery exercises to unleash their intuitive sense. In one case, the group employed such an exercise to help Wink hire a director of operations and management. A guided imagery begins with relaxing the body and letting go of thoughts and feelings. In this state of deep relaxation, imagination and creativity intensify. Participants then embark on an internal journey of discovering insights and information related to a question. For the HOT team, the question was linked to the main topic on the agenda; in this case, the search for a new director. Responses from this meditative state of the exercise can come in many forms—including symbols, feelings, or words—and can be faint or vivid. Participants are encouraged to trust whatever comes, even if the meaning doesn't make sense or seem logical at the time.

Guided imagery exercises cultivate a sense of trust among participants because they encourage everyone to share their ideas—not only through the clear expression of thought but through symbols, metaphors, poetry, visual imagery, physical sensations, and emotions. Each person is valued and all modes of learning are respected. The result is a feeling of unity; heightened creativity; and a thoughtful, inclusive decision-making process.

Often people experience the group's collective consciousness and shared leadership after a guided imagery. One IONS participant who led a meditation said, "I felt the group carrying the responsibility for leading the meditation. This was a strange experience. I was supposed to be the leader leading. I got panicky and lost my centerness. Then I had an image——I saw a light connecting all of us. I realized that even though I may be leading the meditation, each person was right there supporting me. It was a good metaphor for how our group shares leadership."

The HOT team's exercise also led to concrete business results: The group not only developed a list of qualities they saw as essential for the new director; they also offered suggestions for the hiring process and ultimately participated in this process.

Through the combination of check-ins, storytelling, and guided imagery, the HOT team developed trust, authentic communication, shared meaning, and purposeful coherence—key qualities for transforming a culture. These capacities and skills can be difficult to master. As one team member expressed it, "Being on the HOT team was very hard for me. It's hard to listen, to talk, and to meditate. It's uncomfortable for me to learn how different other people are from me. I'm learning to trust the process we are all going through at IONS, and I've grown a lot."

Facing the Challenges of Change

As new ways of conducting meetings and making decisions spread throughout IONS, several challenges arose that made the learning journey particularly difficult.

Living with Paradox. The HOT team had major responsibilities for a number of IONS programs. In meetings, participants often struggled with balancing the need to "get things done" and the need to let their learning process unfold at its own pace. "When are we going to talk about our tasks?" asked one HOT team member. This same member then went on to say, "I realized that this may not be what this team is about. Something very different happens in the space and silence created here that gives permission for each person to speak to where they are in a given moment. There is something about the whole process IONS is going through that becomes known in our meetings. This feels like the 'pulse' of the Institute. . . . What we are seeing is the reflection of the collective psyche of the IONS. I think this is very important."

The team lived with this tension, learning to stay with what had heart and meaning for them, and trusting that the process would lead to results. The insights they gained from this process rippled into other areas of the organization, influencing the ideas explored in the ongoing conversation about the change initiative and subtly reshaping leadership styles. Individuals developed skills and confidence in leading intuitive processes such as check-ins, storytelling, and guided imagery at other staff functions. Cooperation among departments increased because of individuals' experiences on the HOT team. These changes significantly supported the overall learning initiative.

Depths of Despair: The Death of a President and the Emergence of a New Leadership Paradigm. The most difficult time during these three years came with the death of Willis Harman, IONS' highly respected and renowned president. Willis had been somewhat of a father figure for the

IONS staff and a pioneer in the field of global mind change. His death took a huge toll on the staff, not only because they loved him, but because he died before a new vision had fully emerged. Fear and uncertainty about the organization's future intensified.

Wink, now IONS' new president and still CEO, was struggling along with everyone else during this difficult time. Following the organization's tradition, the staff looked to Wink for clarity, direction, and charismatic leadership. However, Wink sensed that this leadership model was no longer appropriate. He deepened his practice—meditating, journal writing, and conversing with people about his and IONS' deepest purpose. He also suggested a provocative theme—*Finding Our Way Together*—for

---

A sense of aliveness and excitement about the organization's future began infusing the culture.

---

the staff's annual retreat. This theme, with its emphasis on the ability of everyone to be a leader, challenged some of IONS' most persistent mental models about leadership. Some people resisted this notion, wanting a strong leader to provide answers. But at the retreat, the staff explored the proposed theme further through dialogue and guided imagery. These exercises, along with Wink's commitment to this new direction of participatory leadership, encouraged the staff to embrace this radically different concept of leadership.

This retreat contributed to the evolution of a new paradigm of shared leadership at IONS. Staff members began readily sharing their ideas, offering solutions, and assuming greater responsibility for outcomes as a result of what they learned at the gathering and at the HOT team. A sense of aliveness and excitement about the organization's future began infusing the culture.

A New Identity Emerges

With any change, losses and letting go are integral stages. During IONS' encounter with the darkest aspects of its existence, with death, and with its crisis of meaning, the staff and board slowly began to clarify their sense of purpose. As the organization's new identity began to emerge, an image of the organization's future also began to unfold—slowly at first, then more urgently, until people began to see and embrace it.

The task now facing the staff was to make meaning of their collective experience and clarify their new sense of purpose. After many attempts and a lot of frustration, the IONS staff created the following purpose statement:

"The purpose of IONS is to contribute to a change in worldview and values that will lead to the creation of a more just, compassionate, and sustainable world through the exploration of consciousness and human potential, and its practical implications and applications for society through inquiry, vision and action."

Partnering with IONS' Members

This statement gave new focus to IONS' learning initiative. It also encouraged IONS to view their membership in a new way—as an active, integral, and central force for accomplishing IONS' purpose of global mind change. IONS realized that many members, through their interactions within their families, at work, and in their communities, were already participating in cocreating a more humane world by using noetic concepts, and that other members were looking for direction from IONS in how to apply noetic concepts in their lives.

This was a significant expansion in purpose from when the organization was founded. At that time, its sole purpose was to support research on consciousness. Over the years, a membership base was established to help support the research program. Communication/education programs were developed later to inform IONS' membership about the Institute's work. To view members as integral to IONS purpose, and to commit to living "noetically," has added rich new dimensions to IONS' purpose and fostered a profound sense of wholeness and integration.

Living Noetically

IONS has emerged from the change process with a transformed culture, renewed energy, and clarity about its mission. The journey was messy, confusing, and decidedly uncontrollable. Yet in many ways, the journey is not over. Indeed, this is a story of ongoing practice, of the need to keep using and applying new knowledge tools and principles and striving for new levels of learning. As one example, the Institute is currently focusing on implementing the vision. As evidence of this, IONS is developing an interactive Web site at which members can actively participate and share their experience with using noetic ideas in their personal, professional, and community lives. Expensive in terms of dollars and time, the new Web site nevertheless reflects IONS' commitment to fulfill its new purpose.

As IONS' change journey unfolds further, the Institute will continue to build on the following powerful results of its effort to reshape its culture: its new capacity to apply its knowledge of the mysteries of the human soul, its clarity about each staff member's unique gifts and contributions, its "noetic" leadership skills, and the community of shared meaning that it has founded by exploring and living its deepest values. ᔆ

Sharon Lehrer is an organizational strategist and leadership coach specializing in collaborative organizational design, personal mastery, team productivity, and community building. For the past three years, Sharon has been the consultant to the Institute of Noetic Sciences on its strategic planning process. She has consulted to businesses, healthcare, government, and service organizations for over 20 years. Sharon has pioneered the use of intuition-based learning methods to address practical and strategic issues in organizations.

© 1999 Sharon Lehrer.

Marion Weber, who contributed the mandala example on page 144, is founder of The Arts and Healing Network Web site http://www.artheals.org and is director of Experiential Learning at The Institute for the Study of Health and Illness at Commonweal in Bolinas, California, where she initiated and developed the group Sandtray, a tool for personal and collective discovery and exploration.

This chapter is excerpted from a longer article. For information about the full version, contact Sharon Lehrer by email at slehrer@nbn.com or by telephone at (415) 461-1860.

Additional Resources

Argyris, Chris, *On Organizational Learning* (Blackwell, 1992)

Dixon, Nancy, *The Organizational Learning Cycle: How We Can Learn Collectively* (McGraw-Hill, 1994)

Senge, Peter et al., *The Dange of Change: A Fieldbook for Sustaining Momentum in a Learning Organization* (Doubleday, 1999)

Senge, Peter, et al., *The Fifth Discipline Fieldbook* (Doubleday, 1994)

Senge, Peter, *The Fifth Discipline: The Art and Practice of the Learning Organization* (Doubleday, 1990)

Other Titles by Pegasus Communications, Inc.

Anthologies
Managing the Rapids: Stories from the Forefront of the Learning Organization
The New Workplace: Transforming the Character and Culture of Our Organizations
Organizational Learning at Work: Embracing the Challenges of the New Workplace
Reflections on Creating Learning Organizations

The Pegasus Workbook Series
Systems Archetype Basics: From Story to Structure
Systems Thinking Basics: From Concepts to Causal Loops

The "Billibonk" Series
Billibonk & the Big Itch
Frankl's "Big Itch" Fieldbook
Billibonk & the Thorn Patch
Frankl's "Thorn Patch" Fieldbook

Learning Fables
Outlearning the Wolves: Surviving and Thriving in a Learning Organization
Shadows of the Neaderthal: Illuminating the Beliefs That Limit Our Organizations

Human Dynamics
Human Dynamics: A New Framework for Understanding People and Realizing the Potential in Our Organizations

The Innovations in Management Series
Concise volumes on the principles and tools of systems thinking and organizational learning.

The Toolbox Reprint Series
Systems Archetypes I: Diagnosing Systemic Issues and Designing High-Leverage Interventions
Systems Archetypes II: Using Systems Archetypes to Take Effective Action
Systems Thinking Tools: A User's Reference Guide

Newsletters
LEVERAGE™: *News and Ideas for the Organizational Learner*
THE SYSTEMS THINKER™